HOW TO
DRINK FRENCH
FLUENTLY

HOW TO
DRINK
FRENCH
FLUENTLY

A DRINKER'S GUIDE TO JOIE DE VIVRE,
with More Than 30 Cocktails Featuring St-Germain

PUNCH
CREATIVE

with contributions by Camille Ralph Vidal

Photography by Lizzie Munro

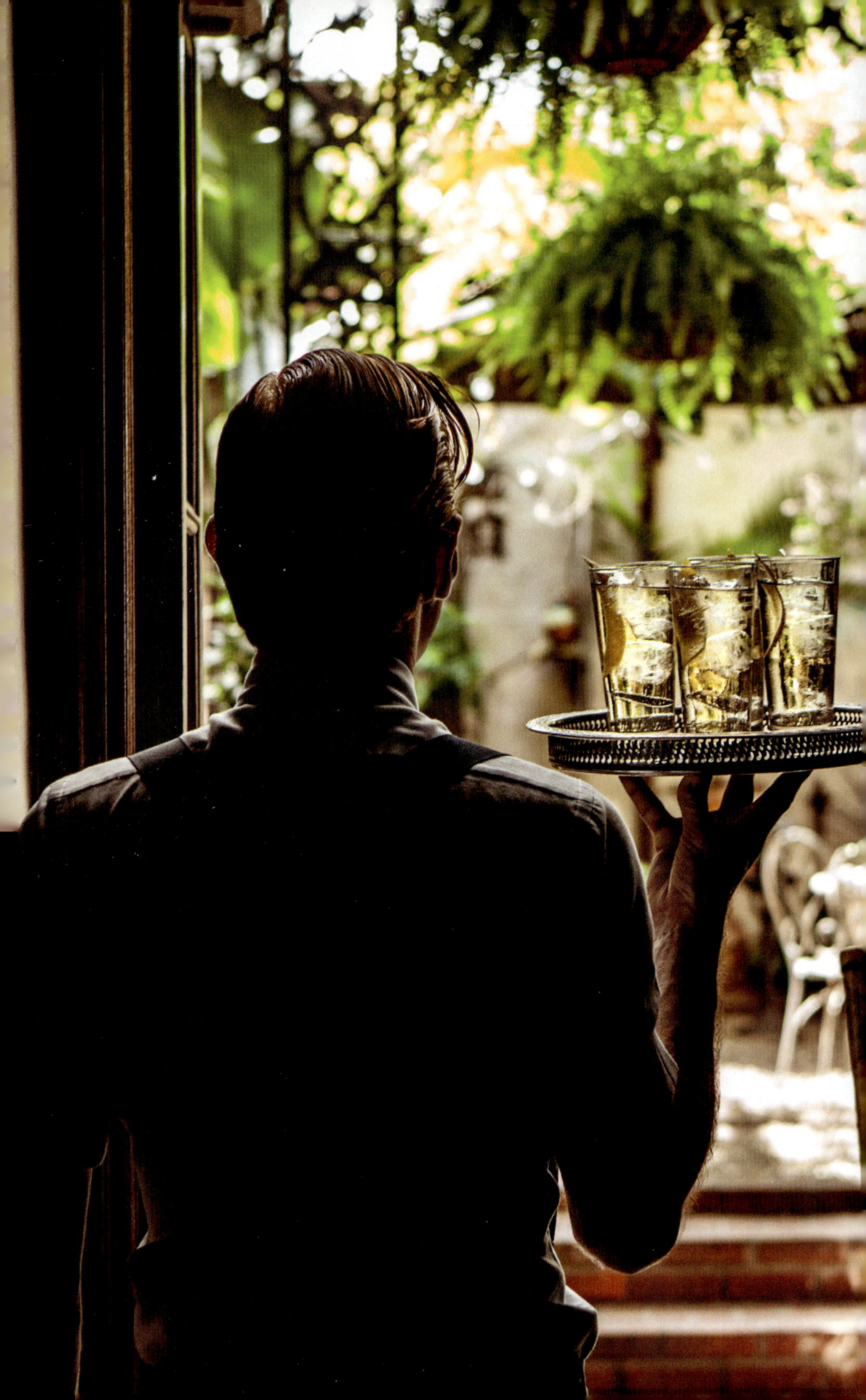

CONTENTS

Index of Cocktails 6 ◆ *Introduction* 9

BRUNCH 13
The Brunch Life 18
Rules of the Brunch Drink 25

DAYTIME 33
The Day Drinker's Palate 40
The Jazz Age Lawn Party 48

APERITIF 57
The Low-Proof Cocktail Movement 68
Rules of the Aperitif Cocktail 75
Aperitif Hour in America 82
Aperitif at Home 92

DINNER 97
Culinary Cocktails 104
Mise en Place 110
Pairing Cocktails with Food 116

NIGHTCAP 125
Anatomy of a Nightcap 132
Building a Nightcap Bar 142

Syrups 150 ◆ *Index* 154 ◆ *Bios* 160

INDEX OF
COCKTAILS

BRUNCH

EAST OF EDEN, Jeffrey Morgenthaler, Clyde Common, Portland **21**

SEÑORITA SPRITZ, Lynnette Marrero, Llama Inn, Brooklyn **22**

TIGER BEAT, Marta Jean Evans, Longman & Eagle, Chicago **29**

GRIEVOUS ANGEL, Laurent Lebec, Big Star, Chicago **30**

DAYTIME

SAN PANCHO, Caitlin Laman, Chicago **36**

SURF CITY SPRITZ, Dan Sabo & Harry May Kline, Ace Hotel Downtown Los Angeles, Los Angeles **39**

FOR REX, Neal Bodenheimer, Cure, New Orleans **44**

NUDIE BEACH, Brian Griffiths, The Broken Shaker, Miami **47**

FLAPPER'S DELIGHT, Julie Reiner, Clover Club, Brooklyn **51**

DA HORA, Ivy Mix, Leyenda, Brooklyn **52**

APERITIF

RIVINGTON PUNCH, Natasha David, Nitecap, New York **63**

C VIDAL, Pamela Wiznitzer, Seamstress, New York **64**

LYSETTE, Franky Marshall, Le Boudoir, Brooklyn **70**

A SCENTED STRETCH, Greg Best, Ticonderoga Club, Atlanta **73**

AL FRESCO SPRITZ, Naren Young, Dante, New York **78**

QUI OUI?, Nico de Soto, Mace, New York **81**

THE SHINING PATH, Will Elliott, Maison Premiere, Brooklyn **85**

GENTLEMAN CALLER, Abigail Gullo, Compère Lapin, New Orleans **86**

THE ST-GERMAIN COCKTAIL, Robert Cooper **90**

TÊTE-À-TÊTE, Xavier Herit, Wallflower, New York **95**

DINNER

VOODOO DOWN, Leo Robitschek, Eleven Madison Park, New York **106**

DARLIN' DON'T REFRAIN, Micah Melton, The Aviary, Chicago **109**

KEYSTONE HIGHBALL, Julia Momose, GreenRiver, Chicago **113**

SMOKED TOMATO, Matthew Biancaniello, Los Angeles **114**

THE HUDSON GLACIER, Jay Bordeleau, Maven, San Francisco **118**

FIORE DI FRANCIA, Ezra Star, Drink, Boston **121**

NIGHTCAP

SAILIN' ON, Karri Cormican, Wildhawk, San Francisco **132**

TURN DOWN SERVICE, Dan Greenbaum, Attaboy, New York **135**

MIDNIGHT BOUQUET, Meaghan Dorman, Raines Law Room, New York **138**

COOPER'S NIGHTCAP, Jamie Boudreau, Canon, Seattle **141**

LICKETY SPLIT, Kimberly Rosselle, Trick Dog, San Francisco **145**

DUBOUDREAU COCKTAIL, Jim Meehan, PDT, New York **146**

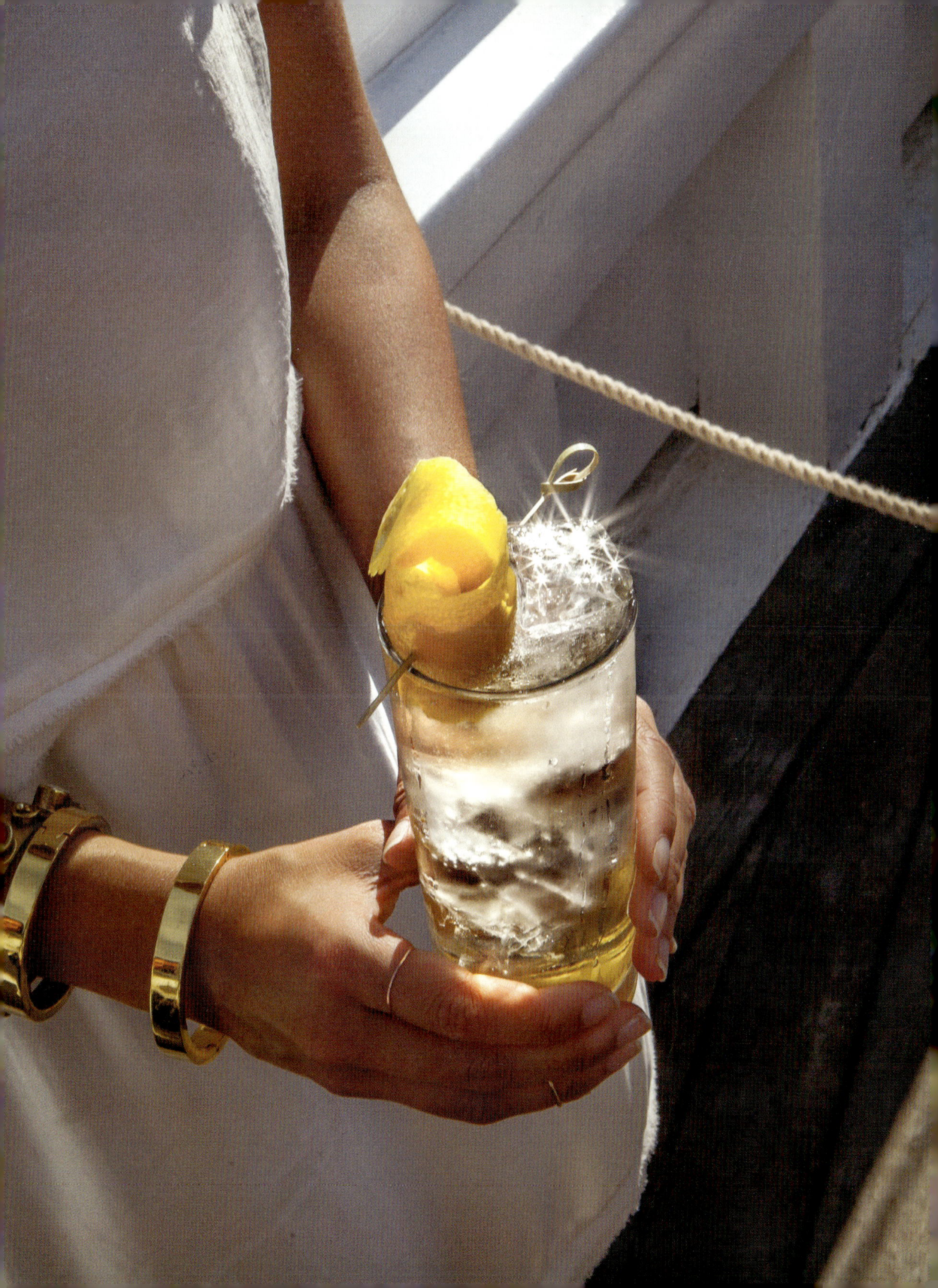

INTRODUCTION

**EVEN IF YOU'VE NEVER SET FOOT
IN FRANCE, YOU LIKELY KNOW WELL THE EFFORTLESS
ATTENTION TO JOIE DE VIVRE MADE
FAMOUS THERE.**

IT'S A QUINTESSENTIAL PART of French identity, a passionate "*Santé!*" to loud conversation and good food, to beauty and taste, to art and music—in short, to everything in life that feels good. For those of us who aren't lucky enough to summer in the Riviera or own a second flat in Le Marais, it's transportive, too—capable of pulling one away from the stresses of the typical day, to a time and place where the present moment is the one that matters most.

In no tradition is this clearer than the *aperitif*, the early-evening custom of gathering with loved ones to share easy-drinking cocktails, light fare, and spirited revelry. "If the happy hour celebrates the end of the day," says *St-Germain*® global ambassador Camille Ralph Vidal, "the aperitif celebrates the beginning of the night." More a way of life than a mere timeslot on a daily itinerary, the aperitif captures what *St-Germain* is all about—elevating and appreciating every experience, no matter how simple it may be. And yet it is far from the only time of day that's improved by embracing this philosophy. The aim of this book is to take you on a journey—from the first meal of the day to the last sip of the night—with *St-Germain* keeping pace every step of the way.

For insight into this French-accented way of life—as well as a number of other topics, such as the balanced art of food-and-cocktail pairings, and the growing relevance of low-proof cocktails here in the United States—we relied on an important group: America's best bartenders, the dynamic and well-traveled tastemakers responsible for getting incredible drinks into the hands of thirsty patrons. Each of the following chapters takes a deep look at a different period of the day, examining how *St-Germain* complements, enhances, and sometimes redefines each. These explorations are accompanied by dozens of original cocktail recipes, showcasing the French elderflower liqueur in never-before-tasted ways.

We start with a look at a great American institution: brunch. As expected at a long, lazy meal meant to loosen us up, the many cocktails associated with this weekend tradition provide ample room for interpretation. Acclaimed bartenders like Clyde Common's Jeffrey Morgenthaler and Clover Club founder Julie Reiner bring us well beyond the Bloody Mary with their sharp, al fresco-friendly additions to the ever-expanding canon of brunch-appropriate cocktails. And because drinking while the sun's up should never be limited to brunch, Dan Sabo, of LA's Ace Hotel, and Neal Bodenheimer, of Cure, Cane & Table, and Café Henri in New Orleans, share tips on mixing the perfect afternoon cocktail—a glorious escape when executed correctly.

As the sun begins to dip below the horizon, the action moves to the aforementioned aperitif, the true heart of the French experience. Here you'll find everything from a clever spritz hybrid dreamt up by Nitecap's Natasha David to a signature, low-proof "suppressor" cocktail from Atlanta bartender Greg Best.

The day then fades into dinner, a ritual that comes with its own set of spirituous beliefs and expectations. Conventional wisdom tells us cocktails don't play well with food—a notion the most cutting-edge cocktail makers in America have all but shattered. In the dinner chapter, bartenders from Eleven Madison Park to Maison Premiere to The Aviary speak not only to the delicate craft of offering cocktails that belong on the dinner table, but to the evolving dialogue between kitchen and bar that is defining some of America's best drinks.

For bartenders and patrons alike, the end of dinner rarely means it's time to head home. Nightcaps, those memorable last-call drinks that send us off satisfied, are a fascinating category, and one ripe for experimentation. Since no one knows how to close out an epic evening better than a bartender, some of the best cocktail minds along both American coasts have offered to show us how to use *St-Germain* in a truly memorable nightcap, turning the default formula—that stronger drinks will put you to sleep faster—upside down.

There's incredible diversity—of style, opinion, taste—among the personalities featured in this book, which just happens to speak perfectly to the French sensibility and its power to inspire and transport, no matter what time the clock reads.

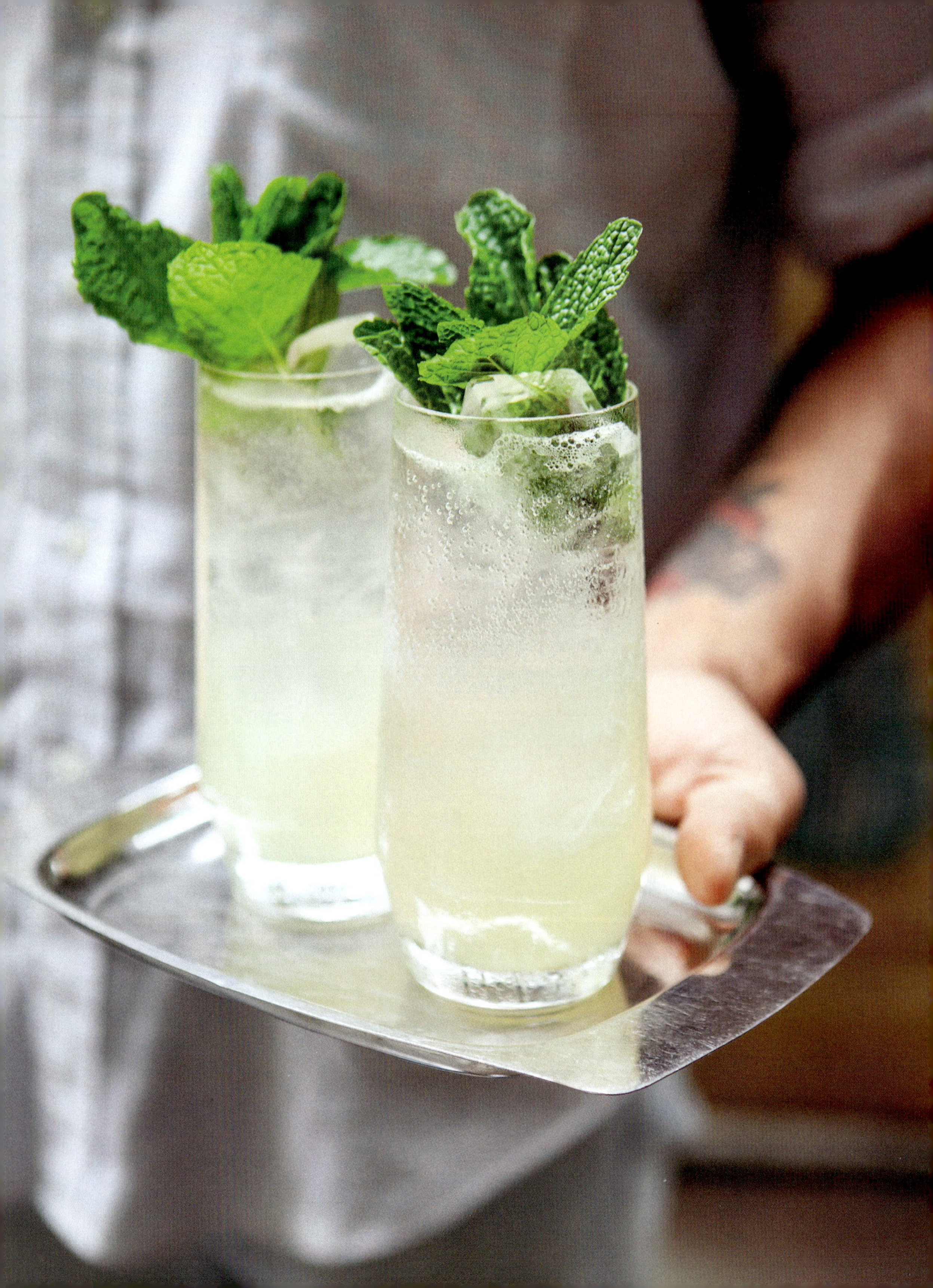

BRUNCH

THE BRUNCH LIFE 18

RULES OF THE BRUNCH DRINK 25

RECETTES

East of Eden 21 ◆ *Señorita Spritz* 22
Tiger Beat 29 ◆ *Grievous Angel* 30

EXTENDING WELL BEYOND THE DOMAIN OF HAIR-OF-THE-DOG CURES AND SPANNING MULTIPLE STYLES, BRUNCH IS NOTHING SHORT OF AN INSTITUTION IN THE UNITED STATES.

THE WORD IS NOT only a noun, but also a verb and, depending on whose Instagram account you've stumbled across, a way of life. It's the late-morning and early-afternoon equivalent of the aperitif: a time to take a deep breath, relax, and reflect on the day—or, in the case of brunch, on the night before.

Well before it became a staple stateside, brunch enjoyed a much more benign reputation in the United Kingdom. Attributed to both the British aristocratic tradition of the hunt breakfast and the family lunches enjoyed by Catholics after Sunday service, brunch was simply a larger-than-lunch spread shared in the daylight hours, featuring some familiar breakfast foods.

The word *brunch* itself first appeared in print in 1895, when an Englishman named Guy Beringer penned a celebratory essay in *Hunter's Weekly* praising the "cheerful, sociable and inciting" custom and its ability to "[sweep] away the worries and cobwebs of the week." It is the cultural imperative brunch represents—the act of exhaling over a long meal after a long week—that has made it more than just a clever mash-up of "breakfast and lunch."

The portmanteau would pop up in print in the United States a year later, in a Pennsylvania newspaper describing the meal as "the latest fad." But fad it was not. Brunch would persist in America as a tradition both social and spirituous—the late-morning train that helped establish the daytime drink in a country still reeling from the so-called noble experiment of Prohibition. "In the early to mid 1900s, brunch offered a platform for people to drink during the day in a socially acceptable fashion," write Roberto A. Ferdman and Christopher Ingraham in a *Washington Post* article entitled "How Brunch Became the Most Delicious—and Divisive—Meal in America."

While the "brunch cocktail" has become as broad a notion as "brunch food," some specific drinks do come to mind. "There are several families when you start thinking of brunch drinking," says Jeffrey Morgenthaler, head bartender at Clyde Common in Portland, Oregon. He designs brunch beverages in five distinct groupings: Bloodys, covering riffs like Caesars, Marias, and Red Snappers; sparkling wine and simple spritzes, like the classic *St-Germain* Cocktail; drinks made with juice; drinks made with egg whites; and coffee-based cocktails. (A sixth category, consisting of beer-based cocktails, such as shandies and micheladas, is becoming increasingly relevant in the brunch realm, too.)

There's supreme variation here, and some drinks, like Morgenthaler's East of Eden—a mix of gin, *St-Germain*, lemon, egg white, and gewürztraminer reduction—straddle multiple styles. "This is the kind of drink that I want with brunch, [and] *St-Germain* goes beautifully with white wine," he says.

A few characteristics—effervescence, fresh juices and herbs, etc.—apply across the board regardless. The most important, however, is a predilection among bartenders for low-alcohol drinks. Why? Julie Reiner, owner of New York's Clover Club and Flatiron Lounge, puts it bluntly: "You want to be able to have a couple cocktails."

Laurent Lebec, beverage director of Big Star in Chicago, looks to the drinking mood of his brunch guests, pacing himself accordingly. While the classic pairing of Lone Star and shot of Old Grand-Dad has its loyalists, others choose to move slower. "People consume early on in a way that [feels] a bit more laid-back and restrained," says Lebec. This leads him to light, fruit-forward preparations, like his Grievous Angel, a bourbon drink tempered with *St-Germain*, strawberry syrup, and lemon. "It's a brunch-ready market fruit sour where the bourbon sneaks up on you in the right way," he says.

No Smoking

Likewise, Lynnette Marrero, beverage director at Brooklyn's Llama Inn, takes into account that many people who end up at her bar early on a Saturday or Sunday are looking to ease their way into the day, and they aren't in a hurry to do it. "You have to consider the state everyone's in when they're coming," she says. She riffs on brunch's two classic revivers: the Bloody Mary and, of course, coffee. Her Maria Sangrienta revises the original with a dose of Peruvian peppers and *leche de tigre*, while her Coffee Buzz commingles amaro and cold-brewed coffee.

Though these bartenders don't get to enjoy brunch quite as often as they work it, they share a similar mentality when it comes to approaching the ritual: A focus on simplicity, and a dose of well-placed restraint, leads to the best results. After all, brunch is a meal meant to be relished. "Unless you want to go to bed early," says Xavier Herit of New York's Wallflower, "make it easy drinking."

THE
BRUNCH LIFE

Why do we love brunch so much? Guy Beringer, the English commentator credited with coining the term way back in 1895, had a few theories. "It is talk-compelling," he wrote. "It puts you in a good temper, [and] it makes you satisfied with yourself and your fellow beings."

More than a century later, Beringer's observation that the ritual is as social as it is satiating is still very relevant. It rings particularly true with bartenders, "fellow beings" who love them some brunch—especially when they're not working it. "A lot of us get into the industry because we're night people," says Julie Reiner of New York's Clover Club. "But all of the bartenders I know love a good afternoon party."

Reiner, in particular, holds brunch in high regard—so much so that she dedicated an entire chapter to the social ritual in her 2015 book, *The Craft Cocktail Party*. Already accustomed to the art of proper day drinking thanks to her upbringing in Hawaii, she made brunch a strong weekly focus at Clover Club. But she is also fond of hosting brunch parties at home. "It's one of the least stressful types of parties to throw," writes Reiner.

Brunch drinks also tend to blossom without much fuss ("Pour some Champagne on it" is an oft-repeated brunch drink motto for a reason). According to Reiner, well-executed brunch drinks "lift the palate in the presence of a meal and are light and balanced enough that they don't impair you."

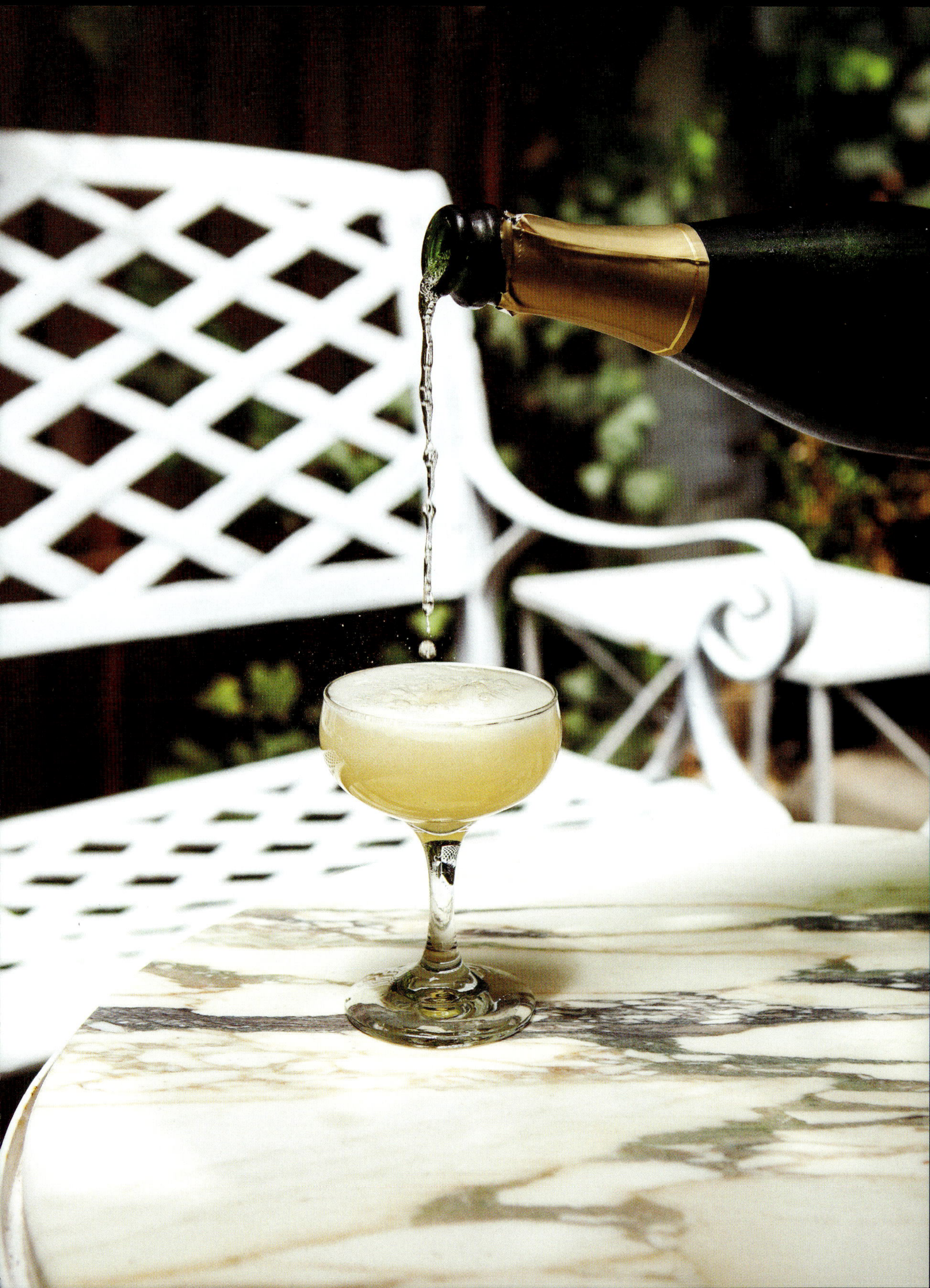

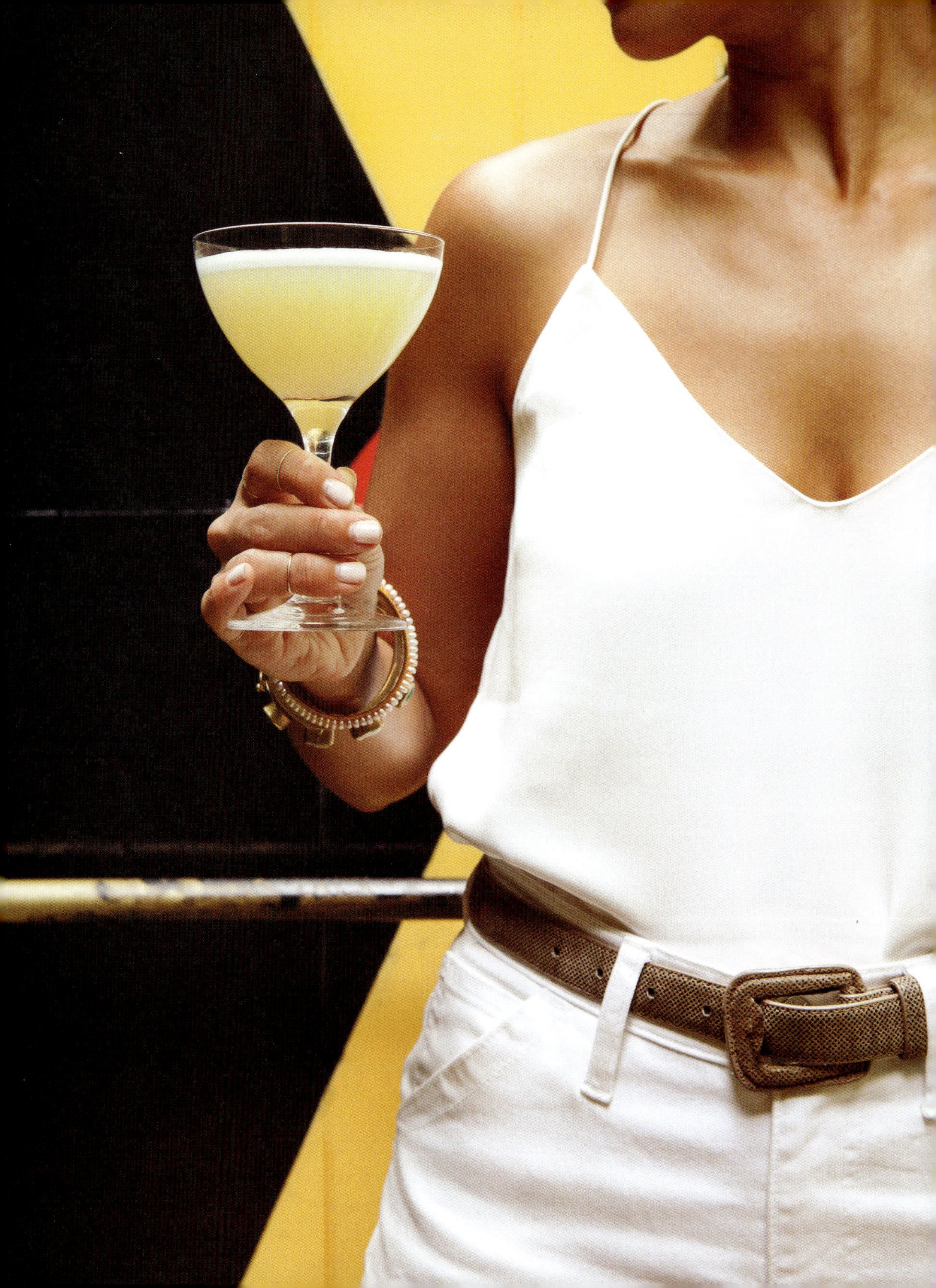

SERVES 1

Jeffrey Morgenthaler
—
Clyde Common

EAST OF EDEN

"I'VE NEVER REALLY UNDERSTOOD the Bloody Mary with brunch," explains Jeffrey Morgenthaler. "It's so heavy." A more delicate alternative, the East of Eden combines gin, lemon juice, elderflower liqueur, and an inventive gewürztraminer syrup. The blend of *St-Germain* and white wine makes for a subtle cocktail to accompany the first meal of the day, rather than take its place.

1½ ounces **London dry gin**
¾ ounce **lemon juice**
½ ounce **gewürztraminer syrup (see page 150)**
¼ ounce **St-Germain**
½ ounce **egg white**

GLASS

GARNISH Lemon peel

METHOD Shake all of the ingredients with ice, then fine strain into a coupe. Express the lemon peel and discard.

SERVES 1

Lynnette Marrero
—
Llama Inn

SEÑORITA SPRITZ

THE SEÑORITA SPRITZ IS a genre-bending cocktail crafted from ingredients whose origins span the globe. Despite the bold base of fino sherry and gin, Lynnette Marrero's take on the brunch cocktail remains light in flavor through the addition of *St-Germain*, strawberry shrub, and a syrup made from *muña*, a mintlike Peruvian herb (dried peppermint tea can be substituted). The result is fruity, fizzy, and food-friendly.

¼ ounce **muña syrup (see page 150)**
¼ ounce **strawberry shrub (see page 150)**
1 ounce **fino sherry**
¾ ounce **London dry gin**
¾ ounce **St-Germain**
2 ounces **cava**
Splash of **sparkling water, preferably Perrier**

GLASS

GARNISH Strawberry and mint

METHOD Stir all of the ingredients except the Perrier in a rocks glass over ice. Top with the Perrier. Garnish with the strawberry and mint.

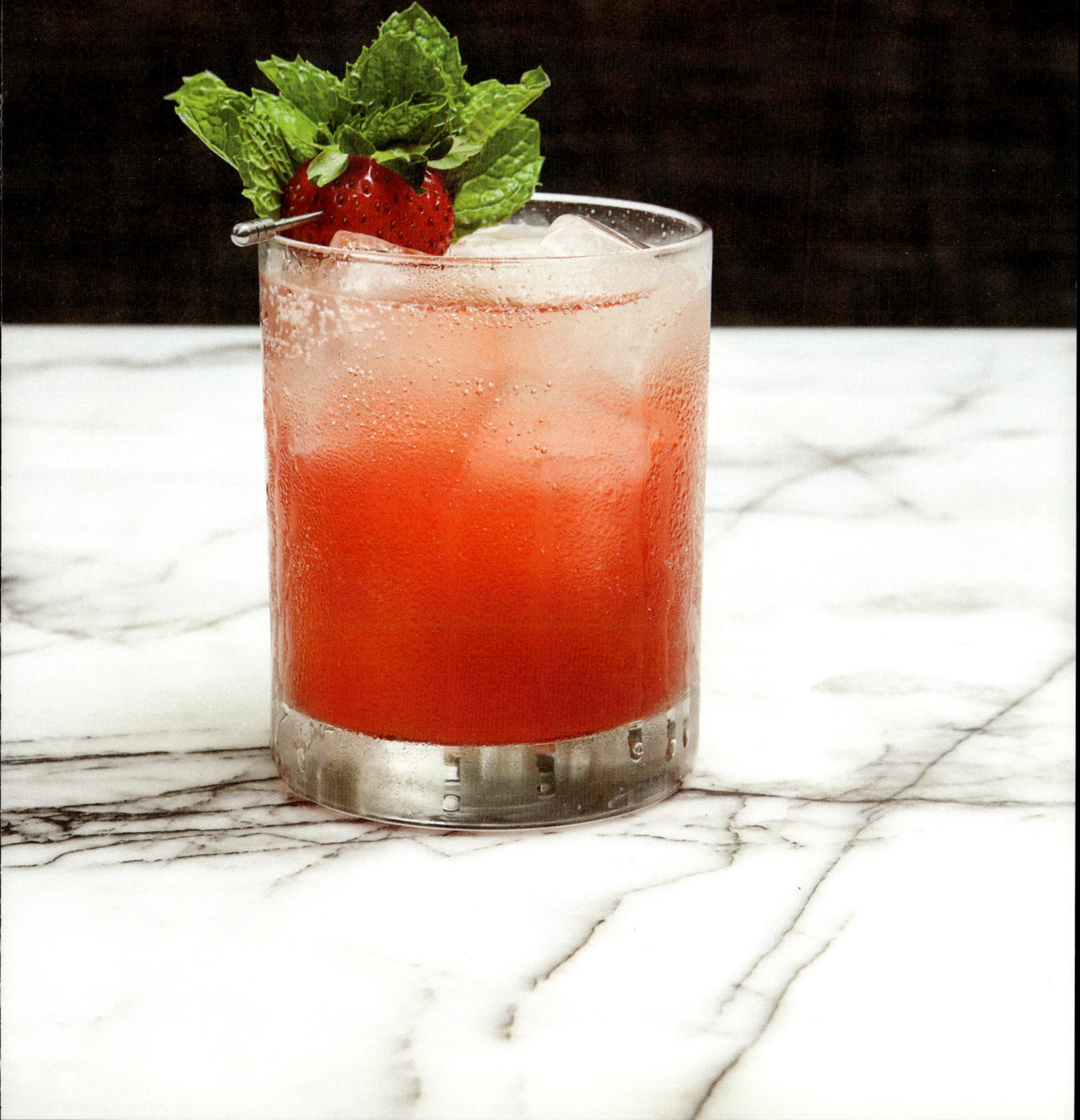

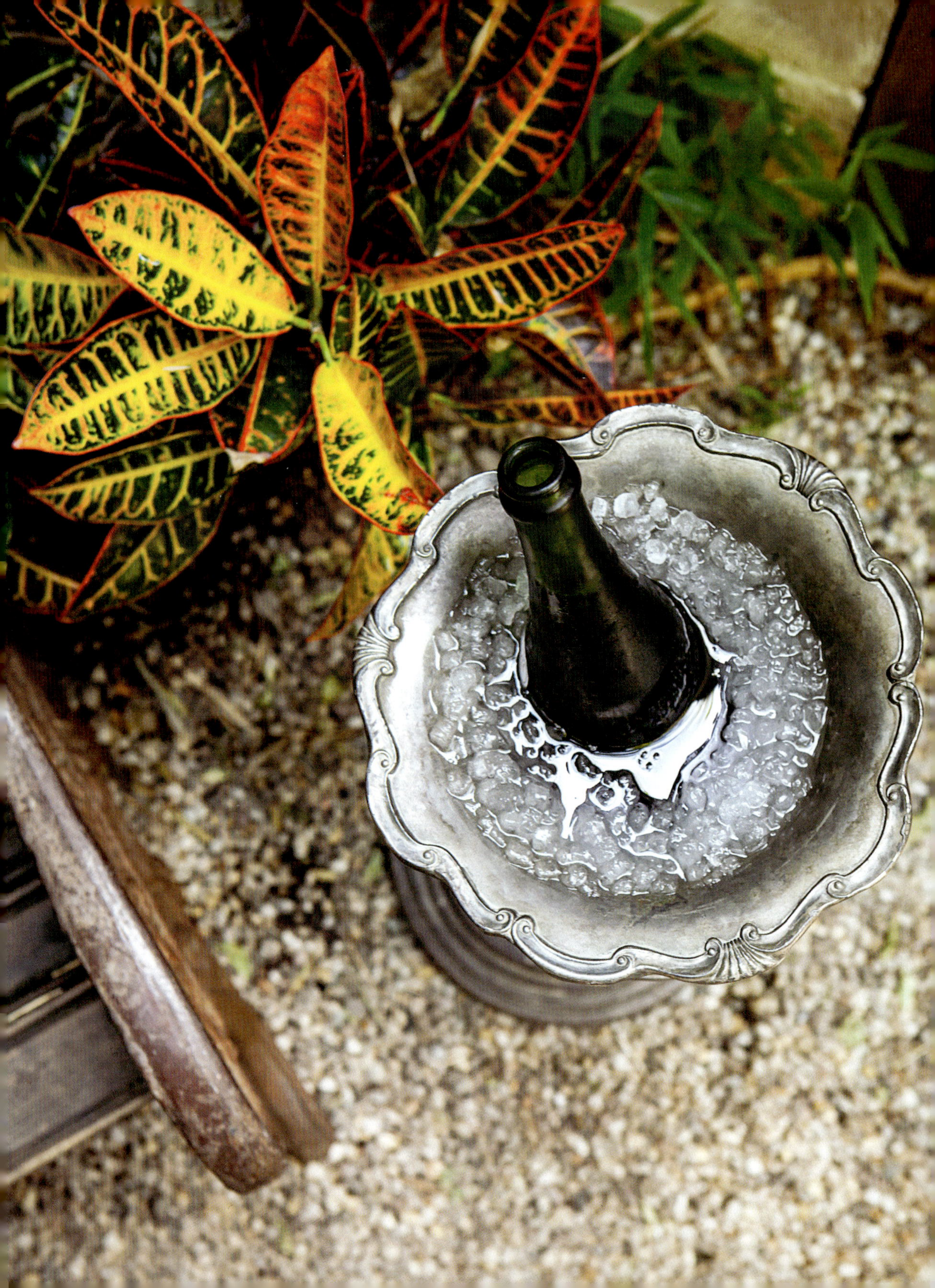

RULES OF THE
BRUNCH DRINK

- **GIVE THE PEOPLE WHAT THEY WANT.** The most persistent brunch-cocktail categories are popular for a reason: they work. There's certainly room for creativity on the service side of the brunch bar, but working within the parameters of classic brunch drinks is a wise move. "No one wants to get into experimental drinks in the middle of the day," says Xavier Herit of New York's Wallflower.

- **BRUNCH DRINKING = SESSION DRINKING.** The leisurely pace of brunch usually means multiple rounds are in order. "You'd like people to have two, three drinks and enjoy—not have one and be done," says Lynnette Marrero of Brooklyn's Llama Inn. "You want to have sessionable drinks on the brunch menu."

- **PUT REFRESHMENT FIRST.** Daytime cocktails can certainly pack a kick, but any teeth should be tempered with the most versatile tools available to brunch bartenders, fresh in-season fruit and bubbles among them. "There's a desire to not have these heavy, clunky drinks anymore. Citrusy, refreshing, sparkling cocktails tend to be very good at that time of day," says Marrero.

- **DON'T EXPECT A CURE.** It makes sense that many brunch enthusiasts are in the market for liquid relief. Don't get too wrapped up in this. "We just make a good drink, and try not to assign any sort of mythological healing properties to it," says Jeffrey Morgenthaler of Portland's Clyde Common.

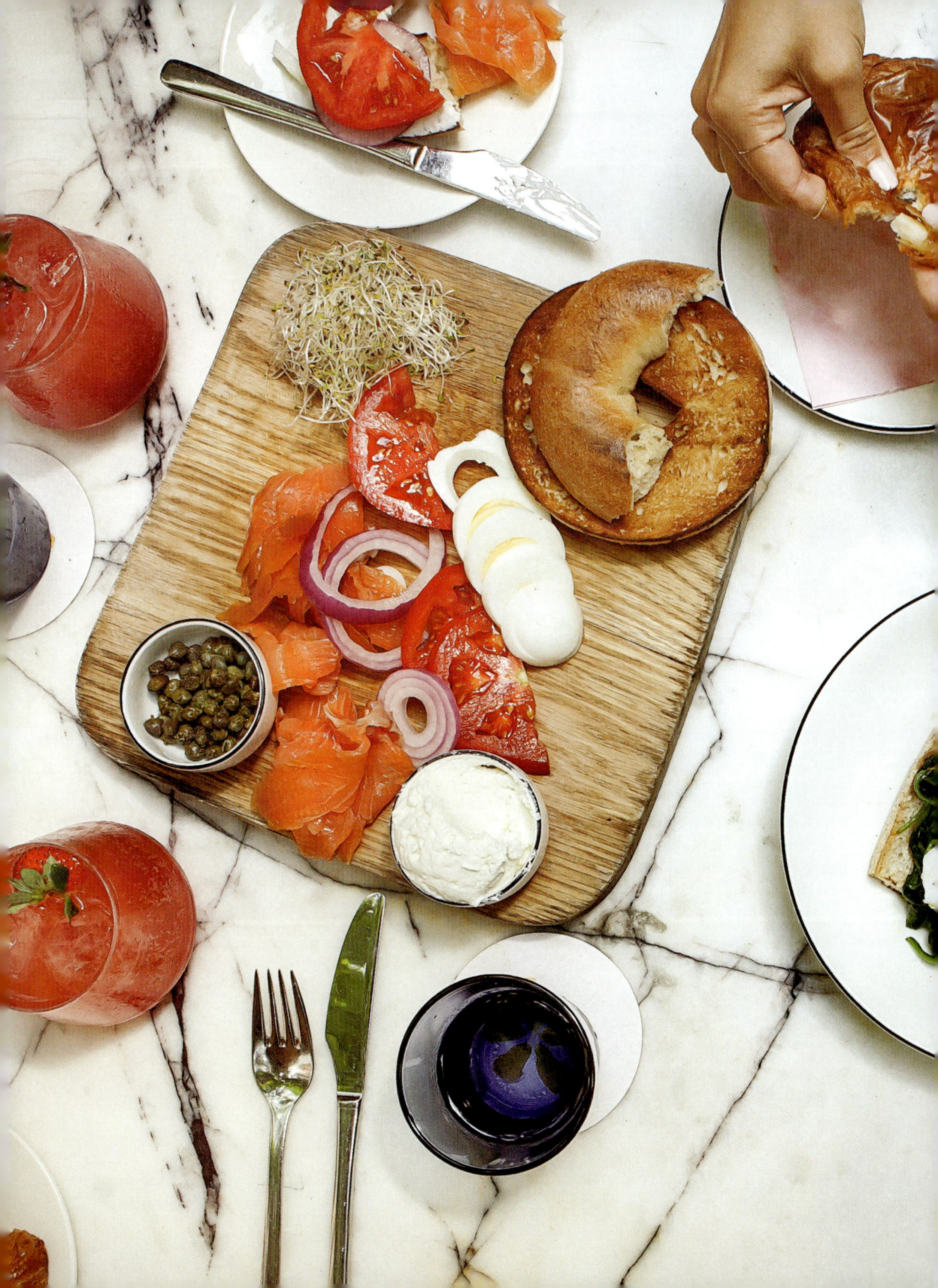

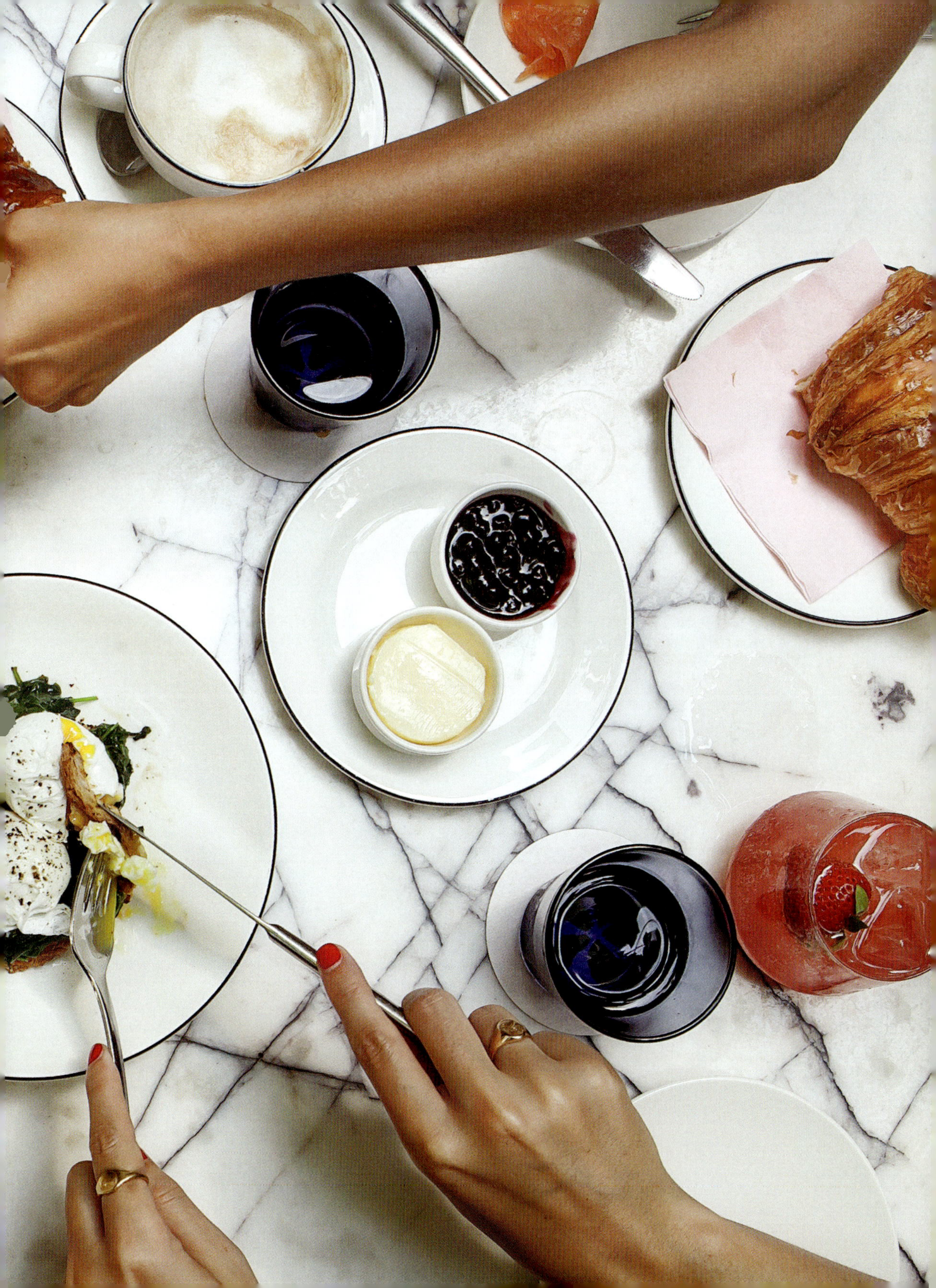

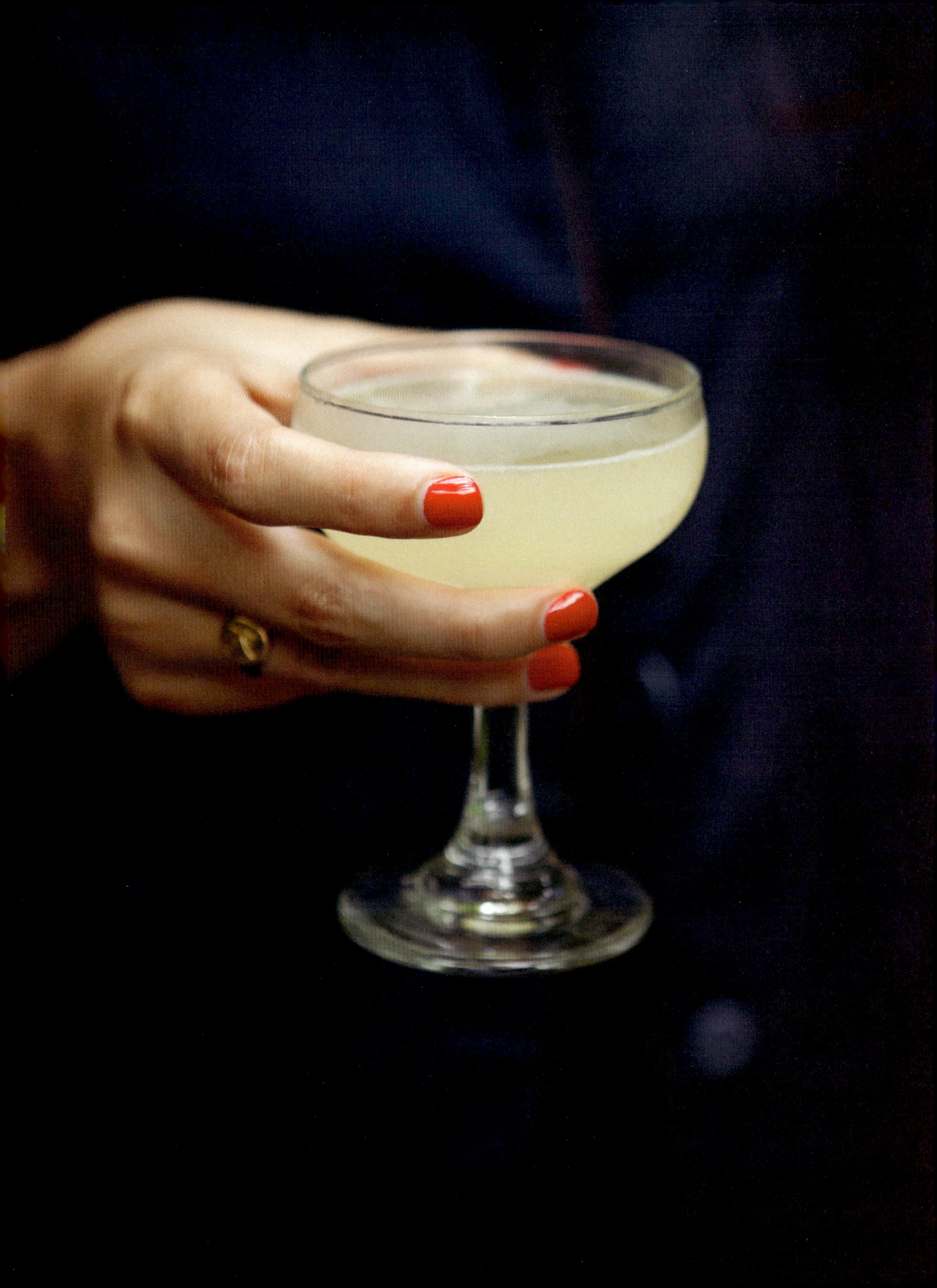

SERVES
1

Marta Jean Evans
—
Longman & Eagle

TIGER BEAT

SLIGHTLY HERBAL AND TART, the Tiger Beat offers just enough kick to jump-start the day. To a base of vodka, Marta Jean Evans adds *St-Germain*, complemented by the fruity, ever so slightly bitter notes of Lillet Blanc, all balanced with the tangy lift of lemon juice.

1 ounce **bison grass vodka**
½ ounce **St-Germain**
½ ounce **Lillet Blanc**
½ ounce **lemon juice**

GLASS

GARNISH None

METHOD Shake all of the ingredients with ice and double strain into a coupe.

SERVES 1

Laurent Lebec — Big Star

GRIEVOUS ANGEL

"ON A SUNNY PATIO, bourbon needs embellishment by way of citrus, bright fruit, or perhaps a floral element," explains Big Star's Laurent Lebec. The bourbon-based Grievous Angel softens the hit of whiskey with a touch of *St-Germain*'s floral sweetness alongside strawberry syrup, and kicks everything up with the addition of bitters and citrus.

1½ ounces **90-proof bourbon**
½ ounce **St-Germain**
¾ ounce **strawberry syrup (see page 150)**
¾ ounce **lemon juice**
1 dash **Peychaud's bitters**
A few dashes of **Angostura bitters**

GLASS

GARNISH Lemon peel, sliced strawberry

METHOD Shake all of the ingredients with ice. Double strain into a rocks glass. Express the lemon peel, then discard. Garnish with the sliced strawberry.

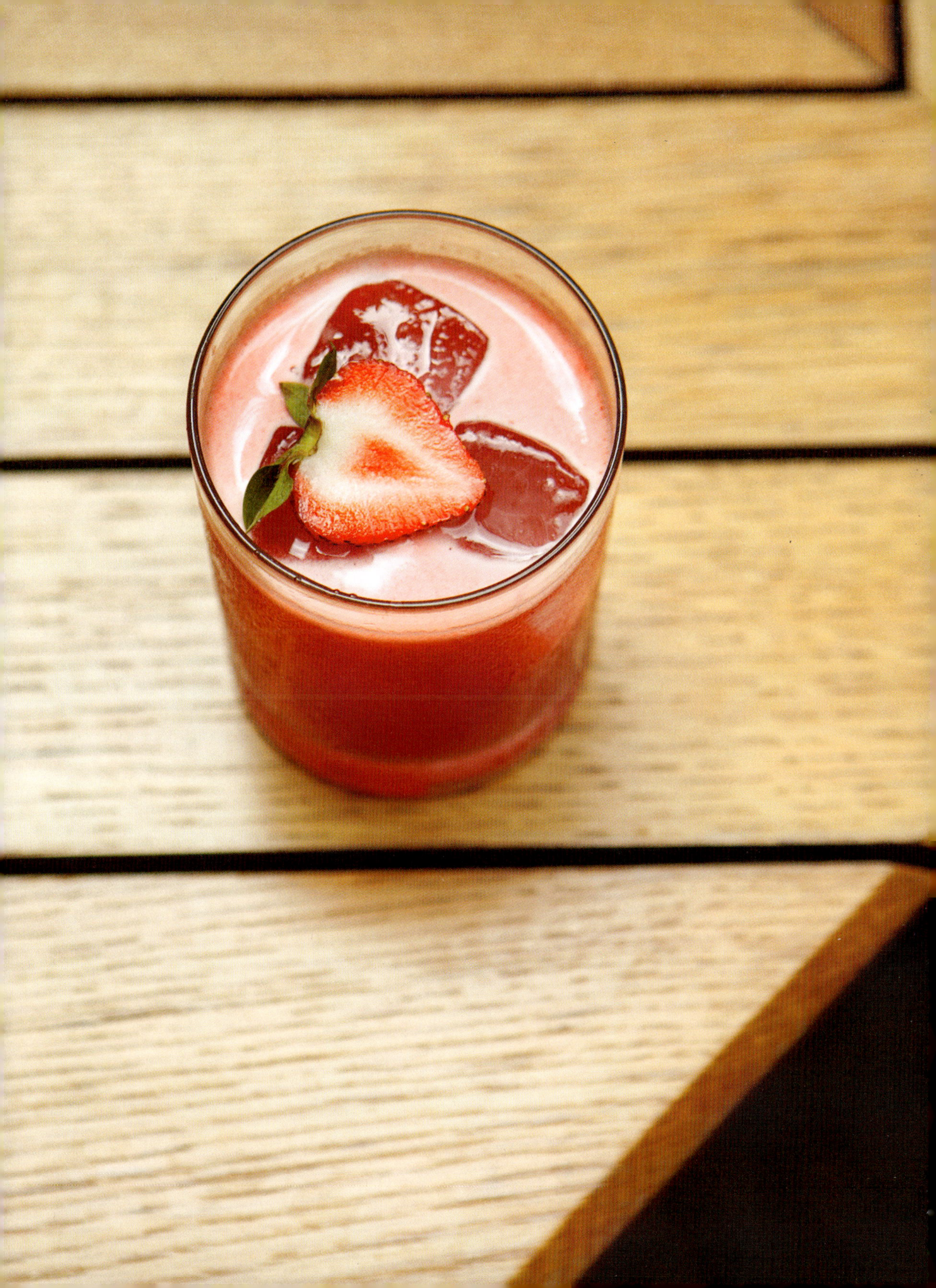

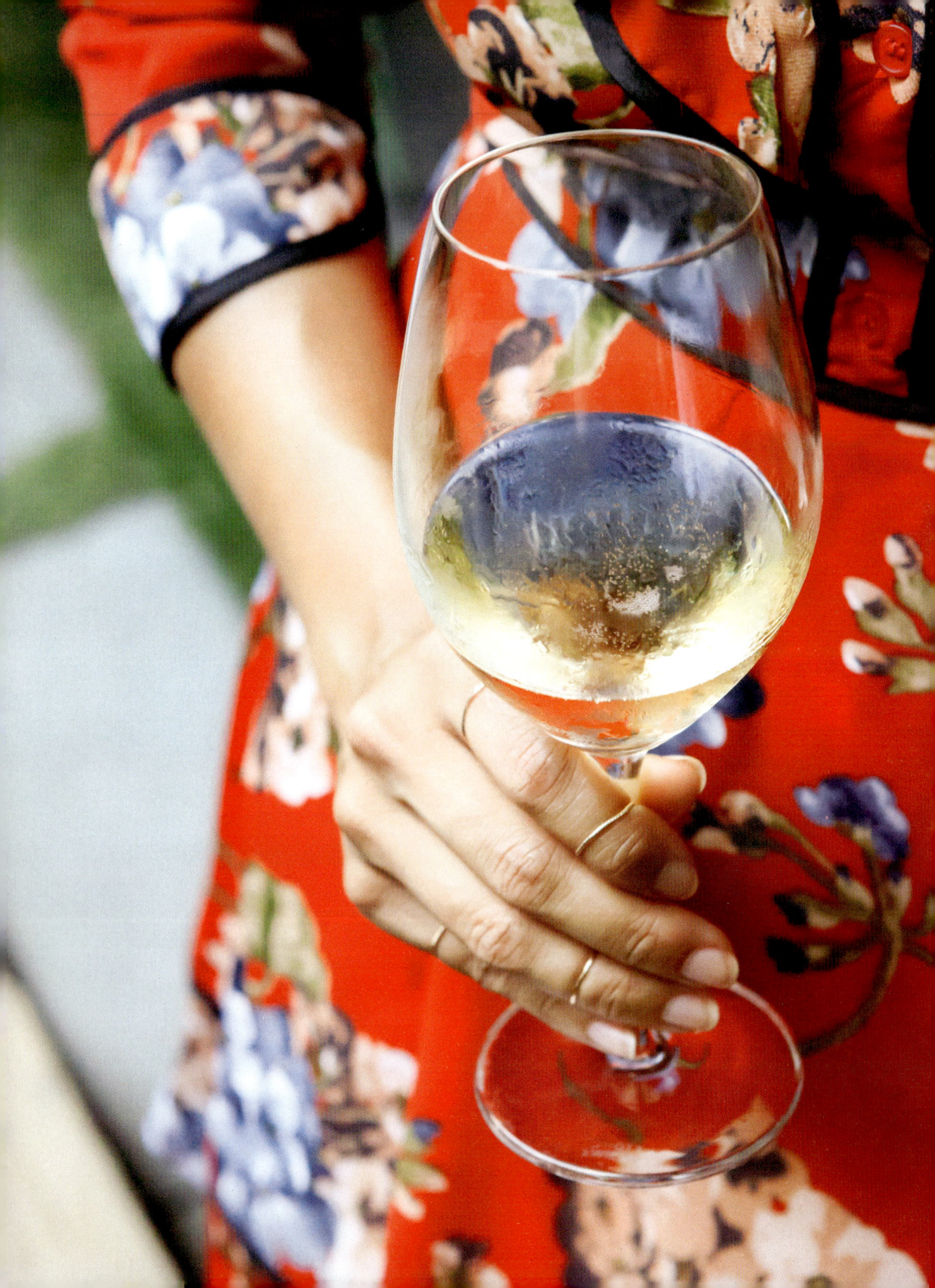

DAYTIME

THE DAY DRINKER'S PALATE 40

**THE JAZZ AGE
LAWN PARTY** 48

RECETTES

San Pancho 36 ◆ *Surf City Spritz* 39 ◆ *For Rex* 44
Nudie Beach 47 ◆ *Flapper's Delight* 51 ◆ *Da Hora* 52

**IT CAN BE AS SIMPLE AS
ENJOYING A BEER DURING AN AL FRESCO LUNCH
BREAK, OR A PLAN TO MAKE THE
MOST OF A SUNNY DAY.**

NO MATTER THE SITUATION, day drinking is a joyous practice for those who know how to do it right. Where you are, who you're with, and, of course, what you're drinking shapes the experience into its best form: a spontaneous diversion from the everyday grind, one that refreshes the spirit with a light, crisp drink and a little vitamin D.

Though it may seem like Americans mostly enjoy their drinks after the sun has gone down, daytime drinking has been part of American identity since colonial times, when people would start their days with beers or spirits over breakfast. Still, in recent decades, it's largely fallen on Europeans—specifically in those countries that straddle the Mediterranean—to carry the joie-de-vivre flag for midday libations.

"Anywhere in Europe? It's kind of the norm," says Ivy Mix, co-owner and head bartender at Brooklyn's Leyenda. The deeply held aperitif traditions and sociable café cultures of France, Italy, and Spain are just a few examples of how drinking is ingratiated into the everyday routine. But the day drink is beginning to catch on once again—partly on the coattails of brunch and its attendant cocktails. "I personally love day drinking," says Mix. "I like daylight, I like sun, I like low-ABV cocktails and wine. Day drinking is for me."

Getting on Mix's level in terms of enthusiasm is step one—it's then up to the drinker to identify the proper day-drinking venue, whether it be a bar, a pool, a rooftop, or your backyard. Neal Bodenheimer, partner in Cure, Cane & Table, and Café Henri in New Orleans, follows a very simple philosophy to this end: "[It's] going to a place where you enjoy the outside and you're embracing the day."

The real appeal of day drinking is rooted in its ability to serve as a mini vacation. "It's this idea that you can blow off the responsibility," says Bodenheimer, "and go and do something that's fun during the day, when you'd normally be working."

For Dan Sabo, beverage director of LA's Ace Hotel, "sessionability is really important," highlighting another chief rule of day drinking: You're *definitely* going to have more than one. Inspired by geography, season, and simpler aspects like speed of service (Ace's many frozen drink machines get put to work), Sabo serves a selection of accessible cocktails, including spritz and sour variations using *St-Germain*, to Ace's all-day crowd. "The idea is to keep it really light," says Sabo. "I don't know if I want to sit in the sunshine with a big tall glass of bourbon. That just doesn't make sense to me."

Cocktails designed specifically to be consumed during the day, as you'll find throughout this chapter, all share an easygoing, thirst-quenching character. After all, as Bodenheimer aptly points out, day drinking "can be as utilitarian as beating the heat."

SERVES
1

Caitlin Laman

SAN PANCHO

"MANZANILLA AND STRAWBERRIES ARE very good friends," explains Caitlin Laman, a recent Mexico City transplant by way of San Francisco's Trick Dog, who combines the two for her south-of-the-border spin on a simple Collins. Named after the Mexican moniker for San Francisco (a common place-name in Mexico), the San Pancho swaps the typical gin base for manzanilla sherry to better balance the floral notes of *St-Germain*. Made tall with a measure of soda water, the San Pancho is designed for all-day drinking.

1½ ounces **manzanilla sherry, preferably La Cigarrera**
¾ ounce **London dry gin**
¾ ounce **St-Germain**
½ ounce **strawberry syrup (see page 151)**
¾ ounce **lemon juice**
1½ ounces **soda water**

GLASS

GARNISH Lemon wheel, strawberry fan, and mint sprig

METHOD Shake all of the ingredients with ice except the soda water. Double strain into a Collins glass. Add ice, top with the soda water, and stir quickly. Garnish with a lemon wheel, strawberry fan, and mint sprig.

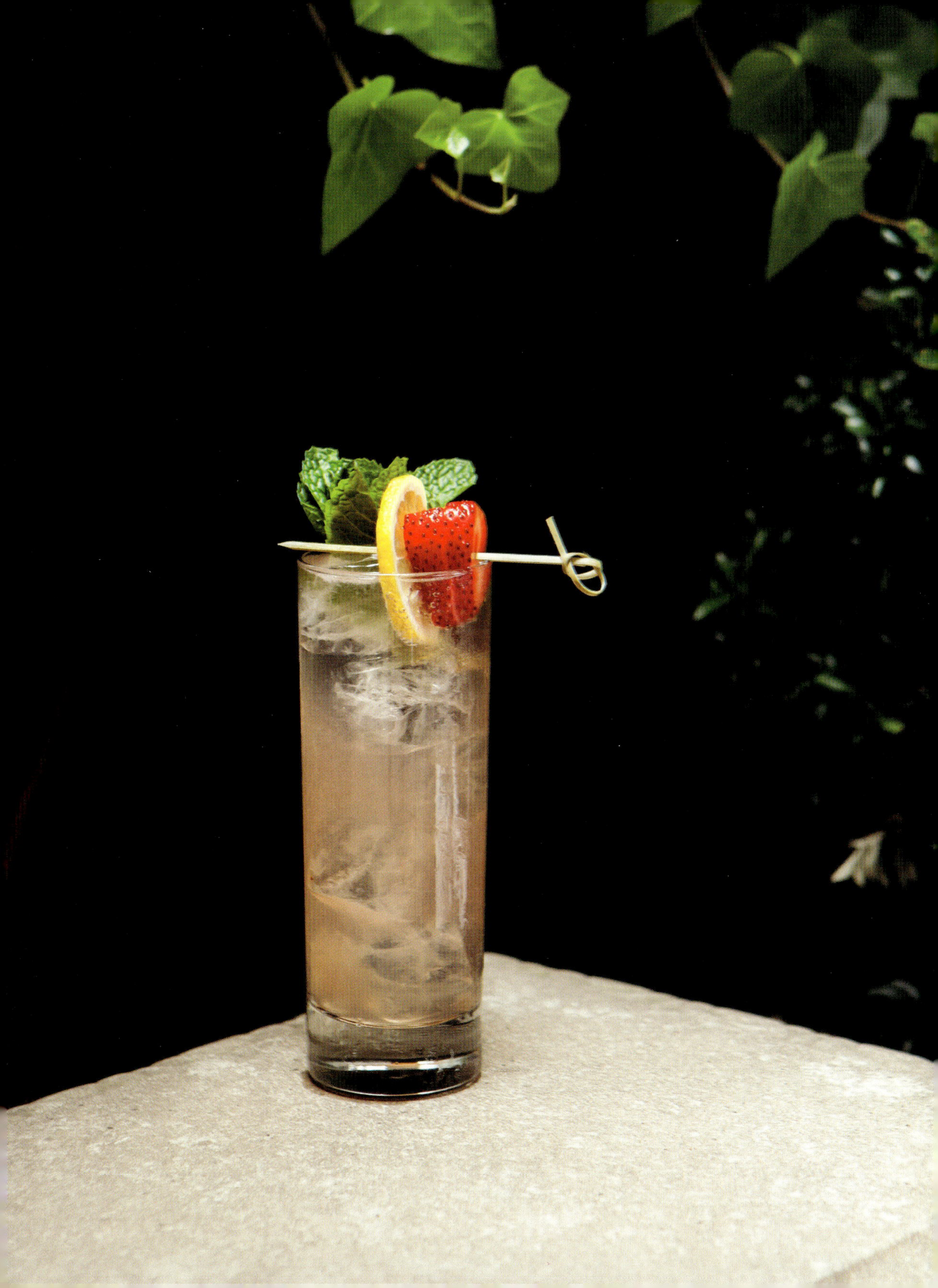

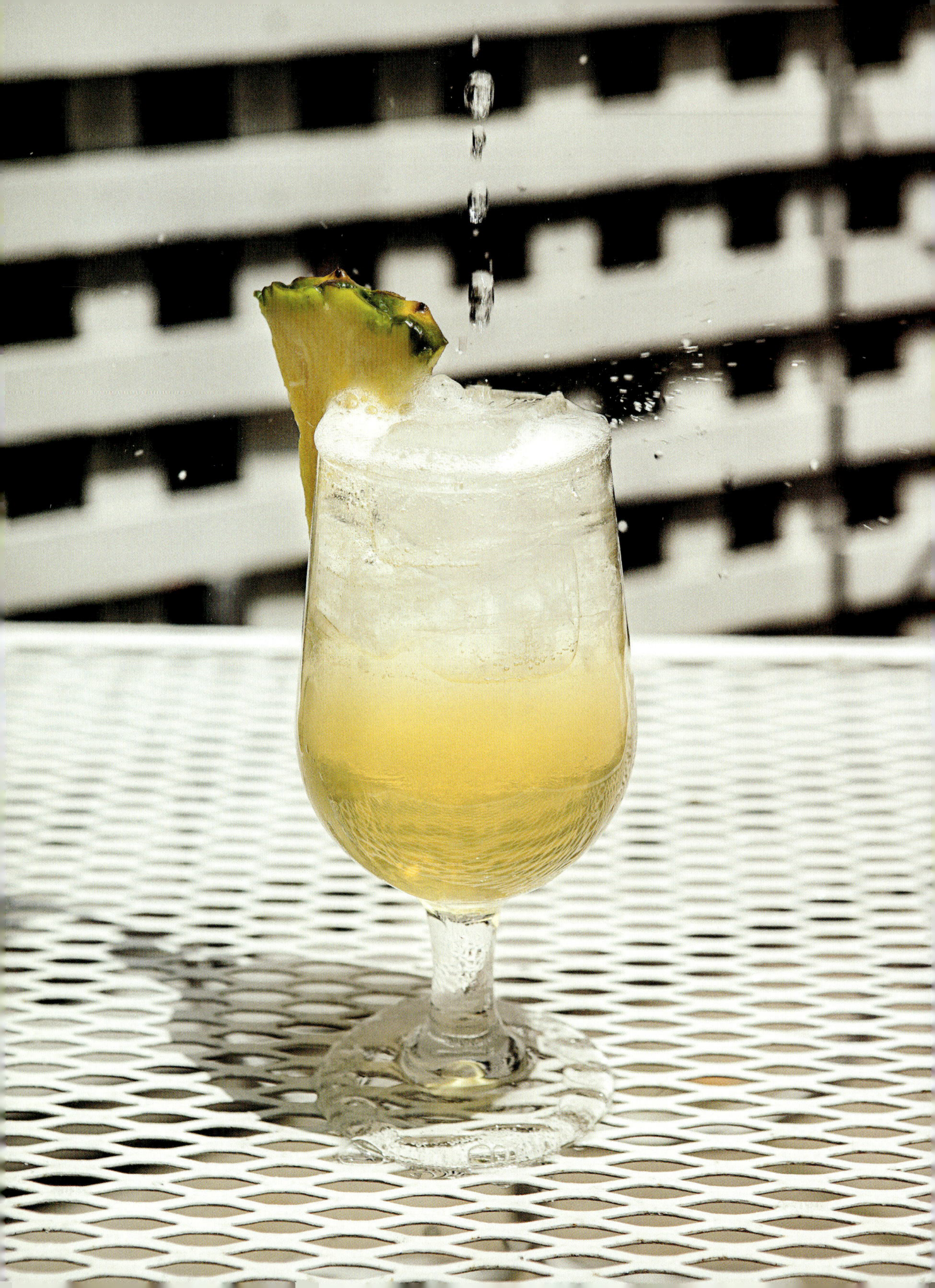

SERVES
1

Dan Sabo & Harry May Kline
—
Ace Hotel

SURF CITY
SPRITZ

NAMED FOR THE SITE of the Jersey Shore's first resort, the Mansion of Health, Ace Hotel's go-to summer cocktail likewise aims to both refresh and revitalize. Crafted from a list of ingredients that includes elderflower, quinine, and nutmeg—all believed at various points in history to have medicinal properties—the Surf City Spritz winks at California's health-conscious culture. While there's nothing actually medicinal about the concoction, the tropical flavors of pineapple, coconut, and honey offer their own forms of invigoration.

1 ounce **American gin**
¾ ounce ***St-Germain***
½ ounce **pineapple rum**
½ ounce **Cocchi Americano**
¼ ounce **honey syrup (2:1, honey:water)**
1 ounce **coconut water**
2 ounces **soda water**

GLASS

GARNISH Dehydrated pineapple chip or fresh pineapple slice

METHOD Stir all of the ingredients except the club soda in a wine glass with ice. Top with club soda and garnish with the pineapple.

THE
DAY DRINKER'S PALATE

The cities where the culture of day drinking thrives are those that require consistent thirst quenching. For Neal Bodenheimer, a partner in New Orleans haunts Cure, Cane & Table, and Café Henri, his home base is among the best day-drinking cities around, thanks to both the weather and the city's quirky architectural character. "One of the things that makes New Orleans such a great day-drinking city is there are so many places to hide out," says Bodenheimer.

It's true that when it comes to day drinking, where it takes place is the most important part of the equation, whether that means a shaded courtyard or a poolside bar. Thus, the archetypal refresher is one that complements its surroundings, and that means a focus on regionality. "I try to think of a drinking experience as transportational, to help you flesh out the scene you're creating for yourself," says Dan Sabo of Ace Hotel Downtown LA.

In health-conscious Los Angeles, many tend toward clear spirits with simple accompaniments. According to Dan Sabo of Ace Hotel Downtown LA, vodka or blanco tequila with fruit and soda, plus frozen drinks and Moscow Mules, are among the most frequent orders.

Bartender Caitlin Laman, who made the jump from San Francisco to Mexico City in 2016, noticed significant differences in the day-drinking styles of those two enclaves. "You see a lot more day drinking in Mexico for sure," says Laman. "It's really normal to wake up here on any given day, have breakfast and drink a couple Micheladas." In San Francisco the general approach to day drinking is subtler. Rosé is among the city's most frequently requested daytime pours, a reflection of both geography and regional tastes.

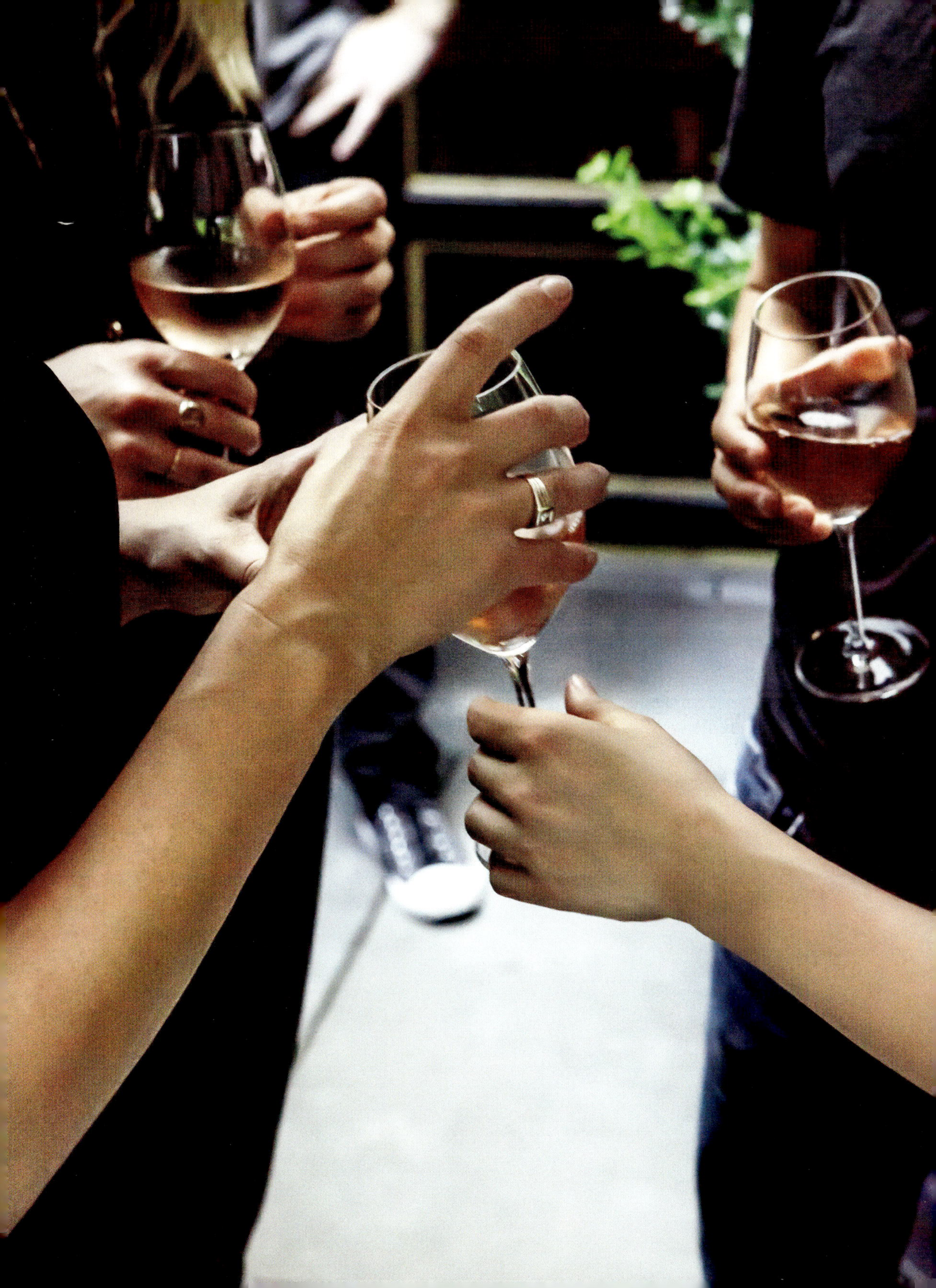

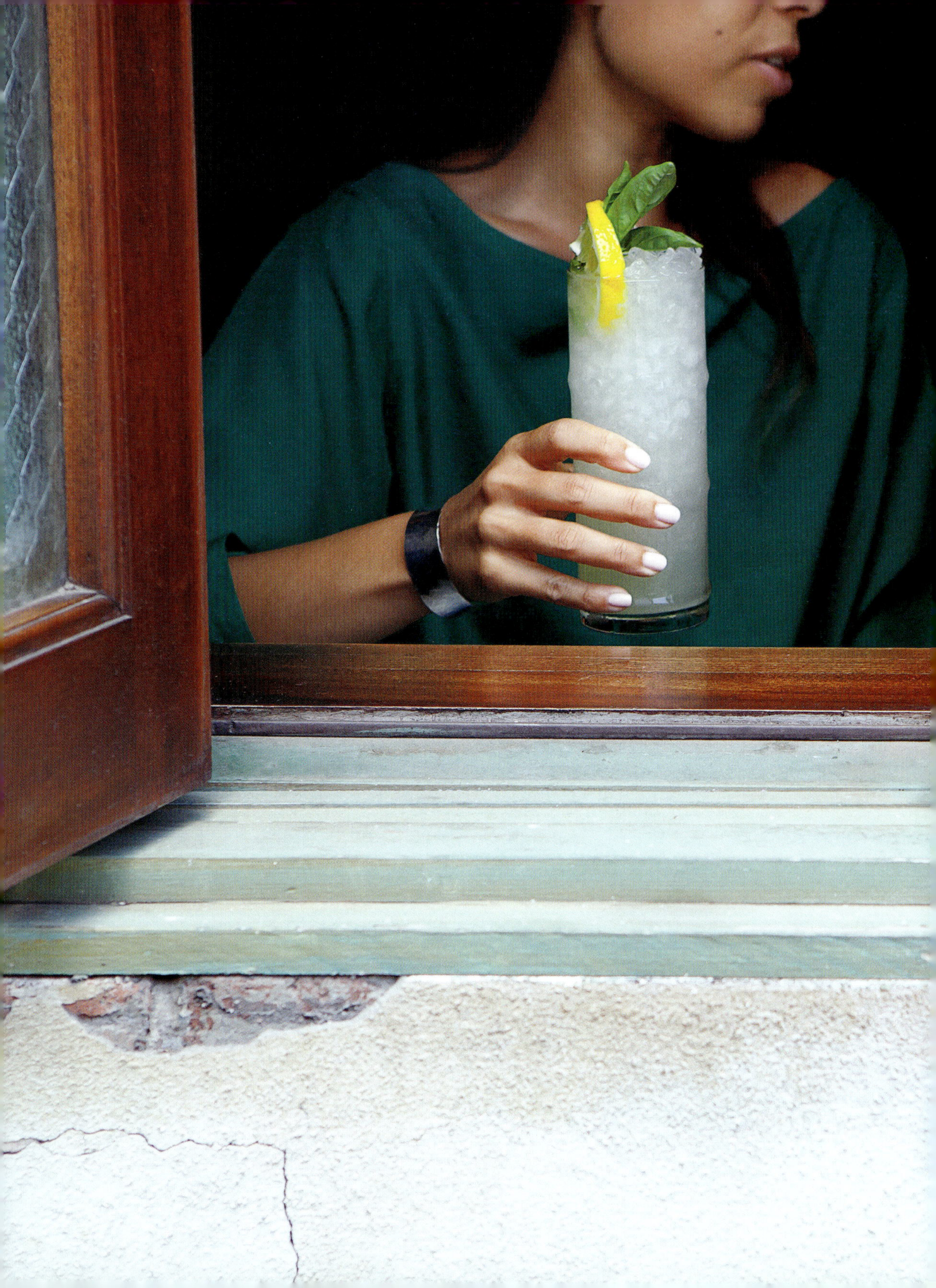

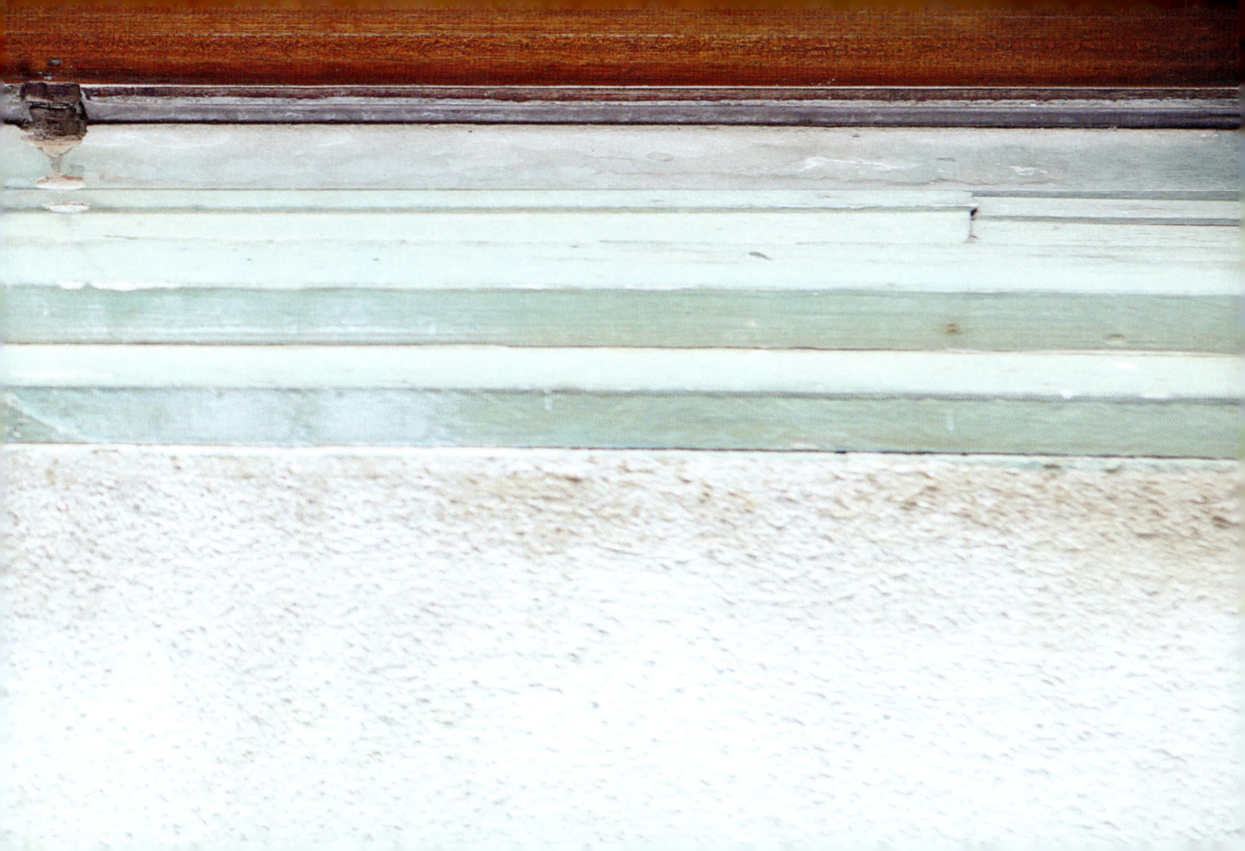

SERVES
1

Neal Bodenheimer
—
Cure

FOR
REX

NEAL BODENHEIMER'S FOR REX pays tribute to his home city of New Orleans and its particular affinity for anise-flavored spirits. Dedicated to the carnival krewe of the same name, For Rex riffs on the classic Ojen Cocktail—a Mardi Gras favorite comprised of Ojen, bitters, sugar, and water—with an added level of complexity by way of *St-Germain*. The combination of elderflower and anise-based Ojen recalls the original recipe for another anise-flavored liqueur, Sambuca, which incorporates elderflower as a major component.

1½ ounces **Ojen, preferably Legendre**
¾ ounce ***St-Germain***
5 dashes **Peychaud's bitters**

GLASS

GARNISH Dash Peychaud's bitters

METHOD Combine all of the ingredients in a rocks glass over crushed ice. Swizzle to combine. Garnish with a dash of Peychaud's.

HOW TO DRINK FRENCH FLUENTLY ◆ 44

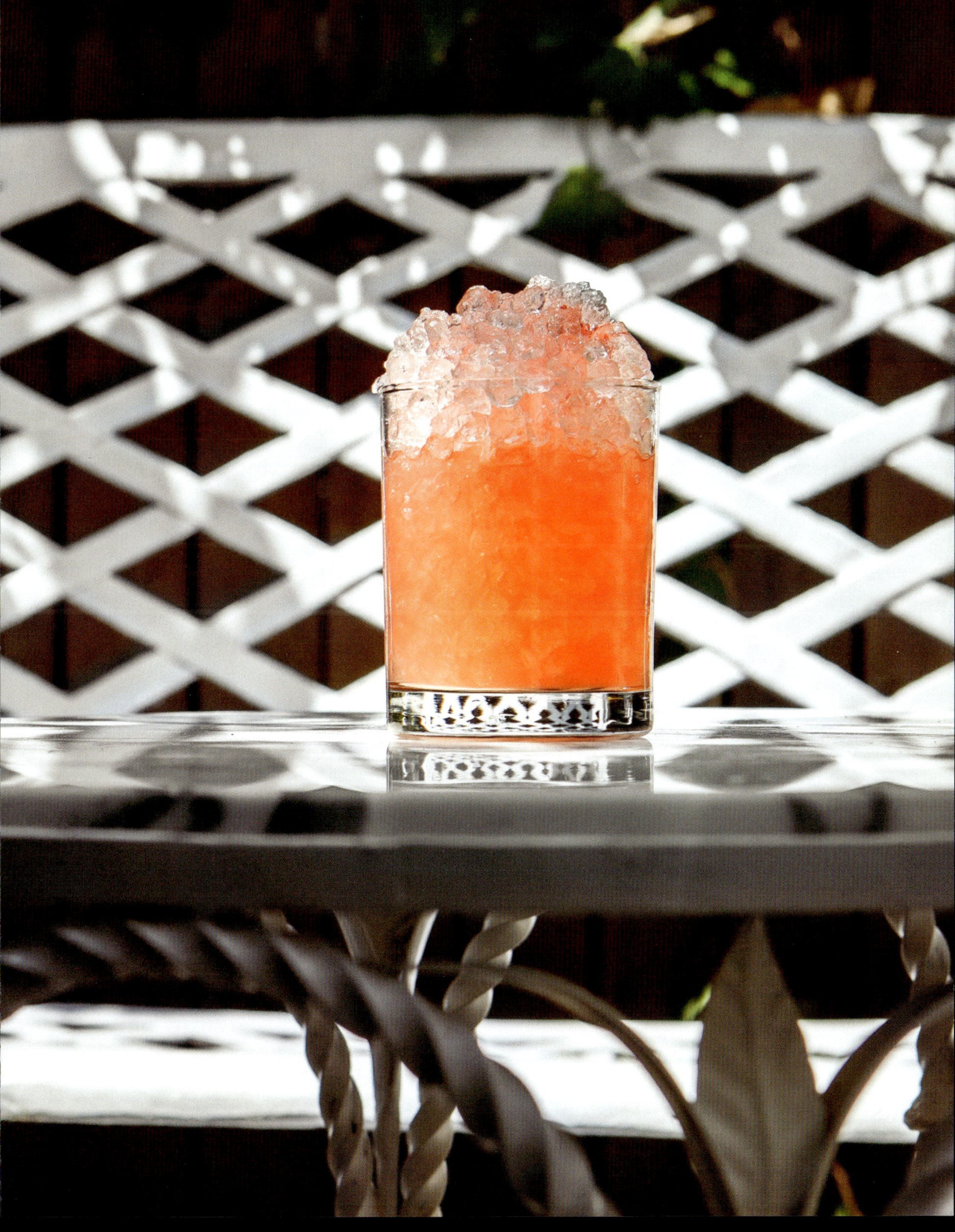

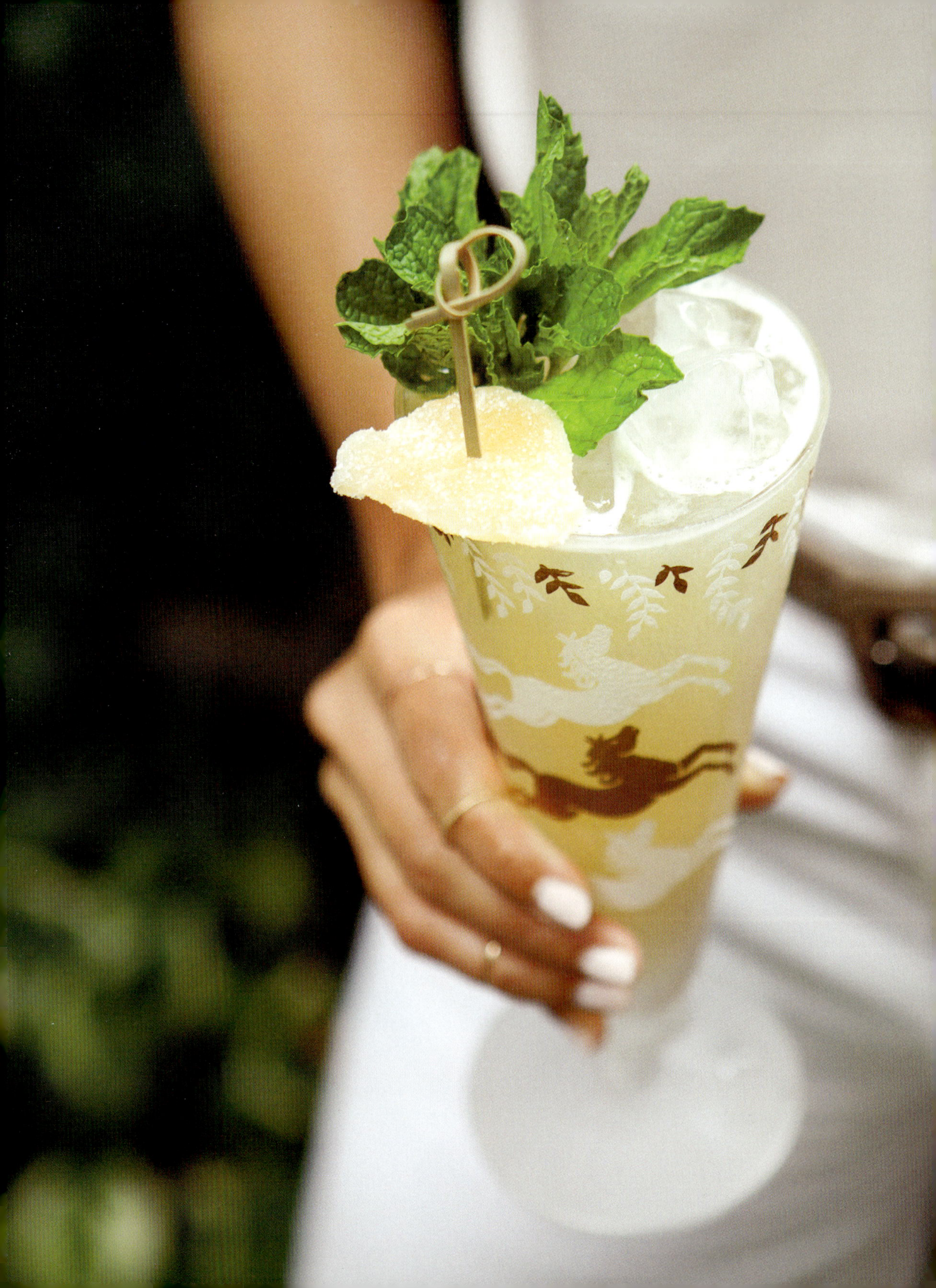

SERVES 1

Brian Griffiths
—
The Broken Shaker

NUDIE BEACH

IN HIS NUDIE BEACH, Brian Griffiths of Miami's The Broken Shaker accentuates the floral quality of *St-Germain* with fresh melon notes by way of housemade honeydew syrup. A dash of rose water brightens things up, while tart passion fruit cools the sweet spice of ginger for a tall and balanced daytime sidekick.

1½ ounces **London dry gin**

½ ounce **St-Germain**

1 ounce **honeydew syrup (see page 151)**

1 ounce **lime juice**

¼ ounce **passion fruit puree, preferably Boiron**

¼ ounce **ginger syrup (see page 151)**

Dash **rose water**

GLASS

GARNISH Candied ginger and mint

METHOD Combine all of the ingredients in a shaker. Shake with ice and strain into a pilsner glass. Fill with crushed ice. Garnish with candied ginger and mint.

THE JAZZ AGE
LAWN PARTY

One of the premier summer gatherings in New York, the Jazz Age Lawn Party has been a one-of-a-kind fixture of the city's social scene since its inception in 2005. Held twice every summer on Governors Island, the event has been produced by musician Michael Arenella since its third year in existence. The conductor and composer's Dreamland Orchestra, specializing in that swinging sound synonymous with the Roaring Twenties, provides a transporting sonic backdrop to guests in attendance, who arrive ready to picnic and dance decked out in crisp, Gatsby-esque fashions of the era. *St-Germain* joined forces with the Jazz Age Lawn Party in 2007, helping fashion the event into an elegant homage to drinking the French way.

Given its theme—to say nothing of the immense, park-covered island the festival calls home—proper refreshments are taken very seriously here. *St-Germain*, in collaboration with Julie Reiner of Clover Club and Flatiron Lounge, offers a selection of cocktails that capture the vintage spirit of the occasion. They're specifically designed with day drinking in mind, light on their feet and thirst-quenching to boot. Take Reiner's Flapper's Delight (page 51), which she lovingly describes as "a real summer porch sipper made for a hot summer day." In many ways, this drink, and the Jazz Age soiree itself, exemplifies what *St-Germain* is all about: a temporary escape from the routine, capable of both refreshment and inspiration.

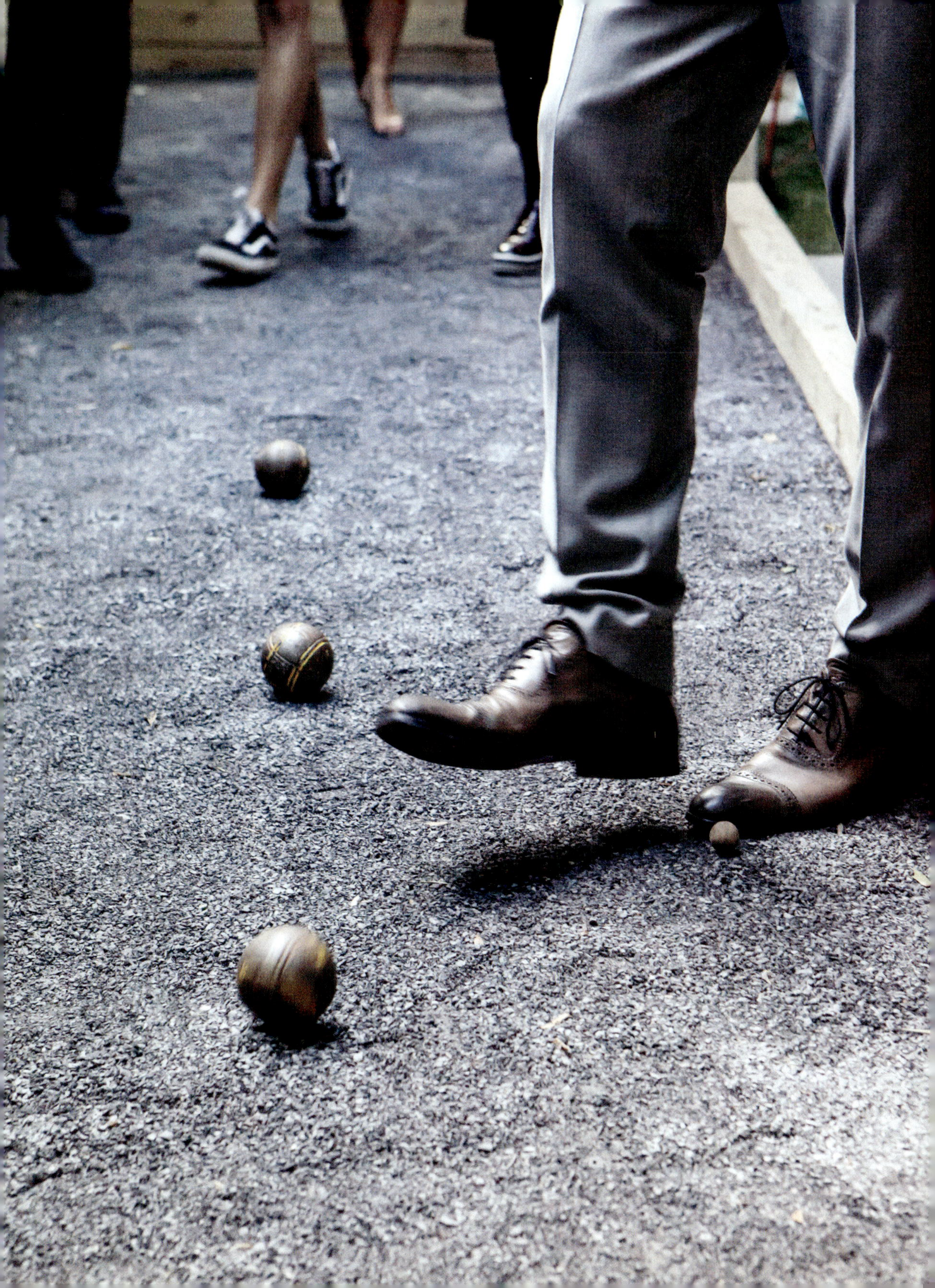

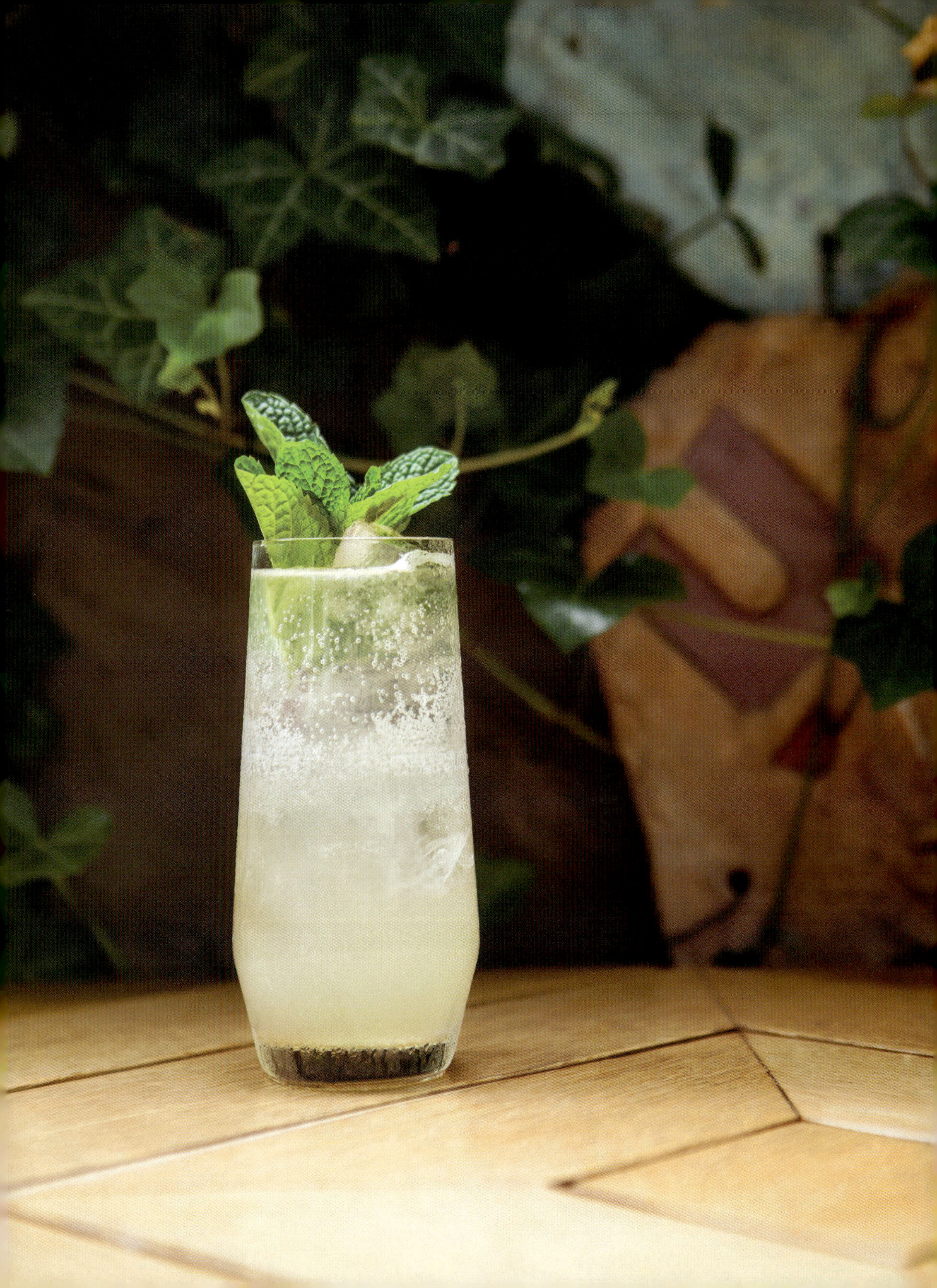

SERVES
1

Julie Reiner
—
Clover Club

FLAPPER'S
DELIGHT

CREATED FOR THE JAZZ Age Lawn Party, an annual summer event that sees the 1920s return in full swing to New York's Governors Island, the Flapper's Delight revisits a timeless combination of elderflower and mint atop a base of gin. Finished with a splash of club soda and a dash of lime, Julie Reiner's thirst-quenching cocktail is a worthy rival to the infamous Tom Collins.

8 to 10 **mint leaves**
¾ ounce **simple syrup (1:1, sugar:water)**
1½ ounces **London dry gin**
½ ounce **St-Germain**
¾ ounce **lime juice**
1 ounce **club soda**

GLASS

GARNISH Mint sprig

METHOD In a shaking tin, add mint and simple syrup and gently muddle. Add the remaining ingredients except the club soda and shake with ice. Fine strain into a highball glass over ice. Top with the club soda and garnish with the mint sprig.

SERVES 1

Ivy Mix — Leyenda

DA HORA

"I WANTED TO MAKE a Latin-inspired royale," explains Ivy Mix of the effervescent inspiration behind her Da Hora cocktail. Utilizing *St-Germain* as a base rather than a modifier, the Da Hora is light, citrusy, and floral-forward, making for a day drink that finds itself somewhere between a Caipirinha and a simple royale or spritz.

1½ ounces **St-Germain**
1 ounce **cachaça**
½ ounce **lemon juice**
½ ounce **grapefruit juice**
2 ounces **cava, to top**

GLASS

GARNISH Cucumber wheel

METHOD Shake all of the ingredients, except the cava, with ice. Strain into a coupe and top with the cava, then garnish with the cucumber wheel.

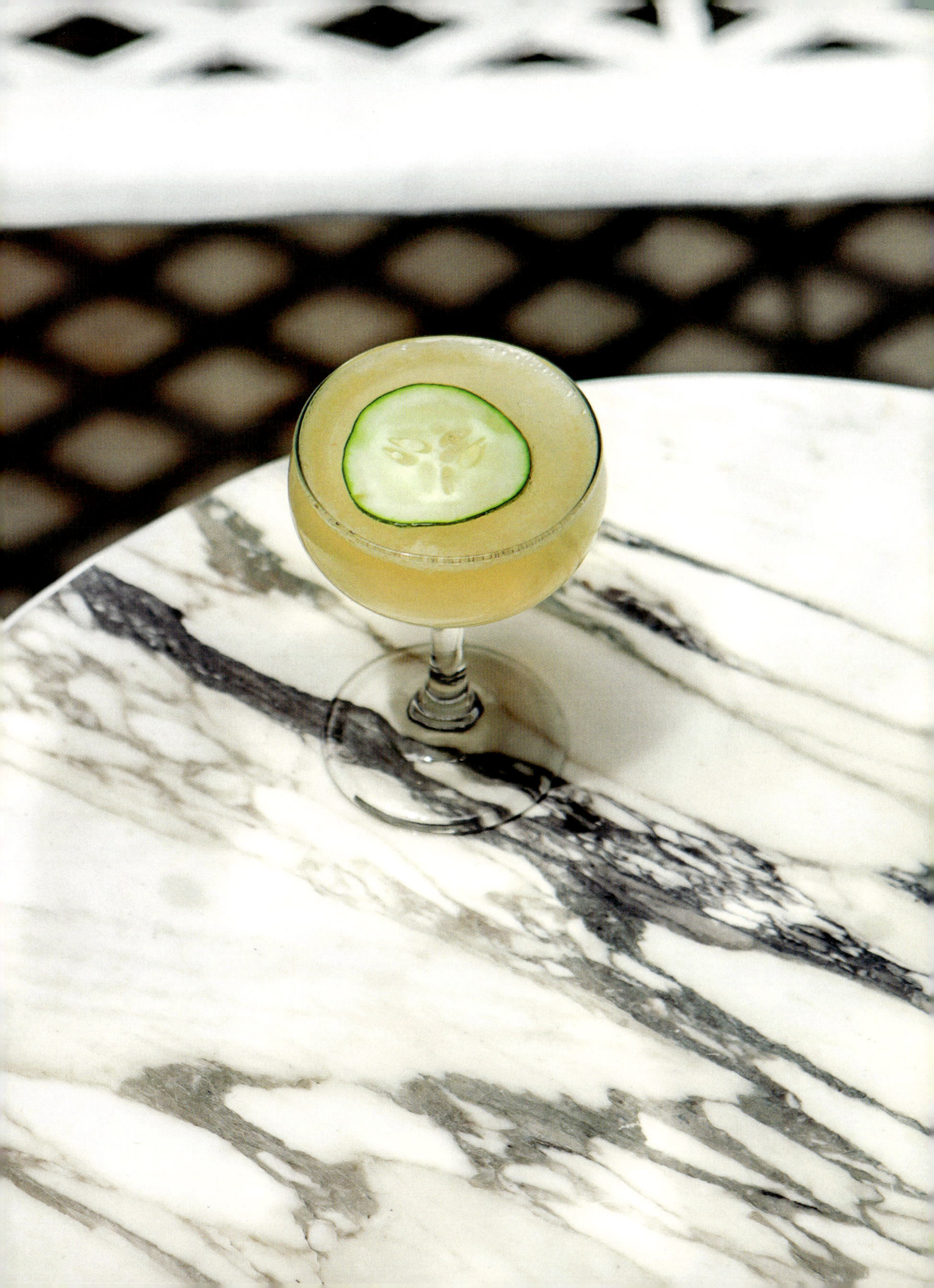

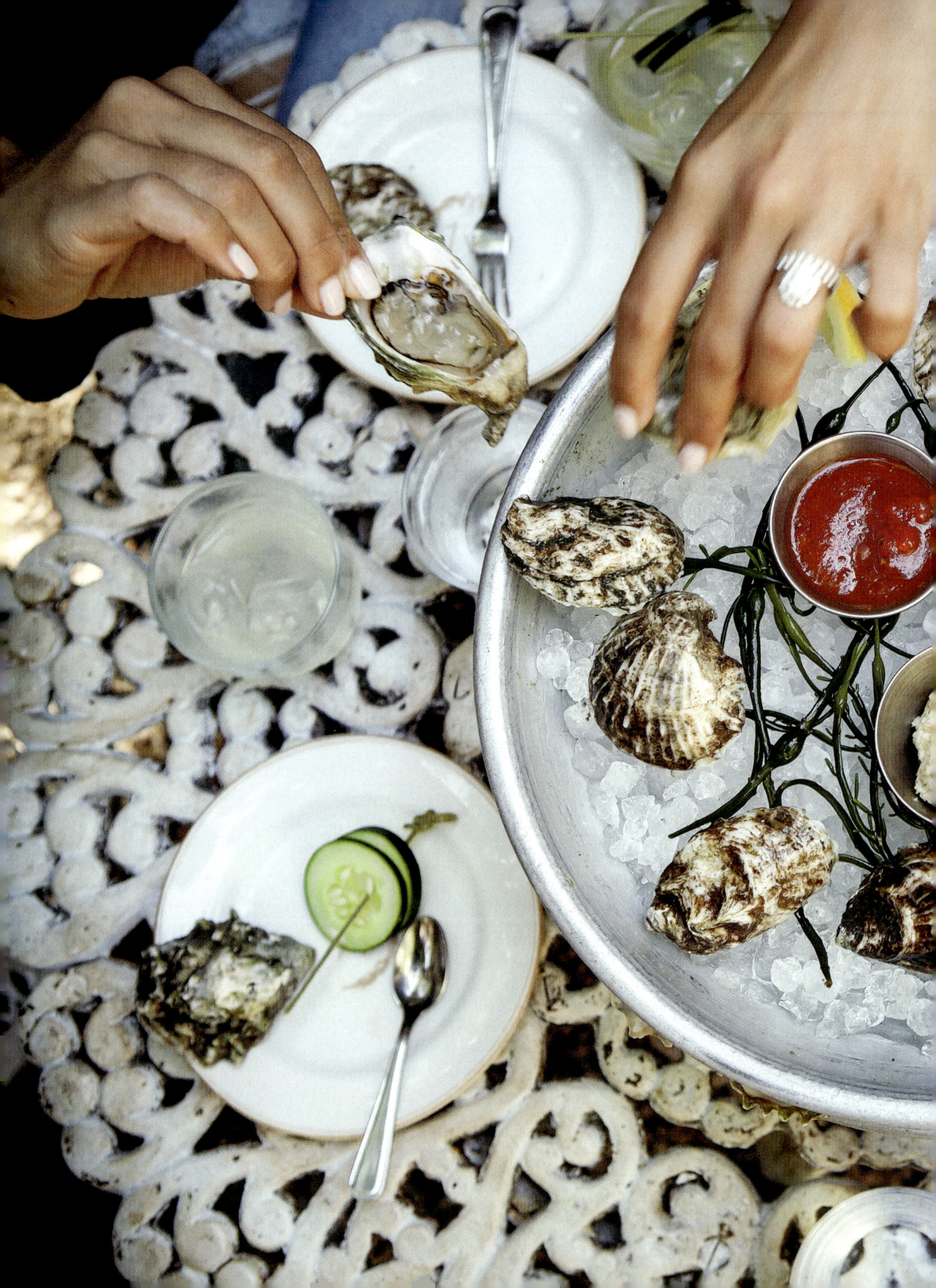

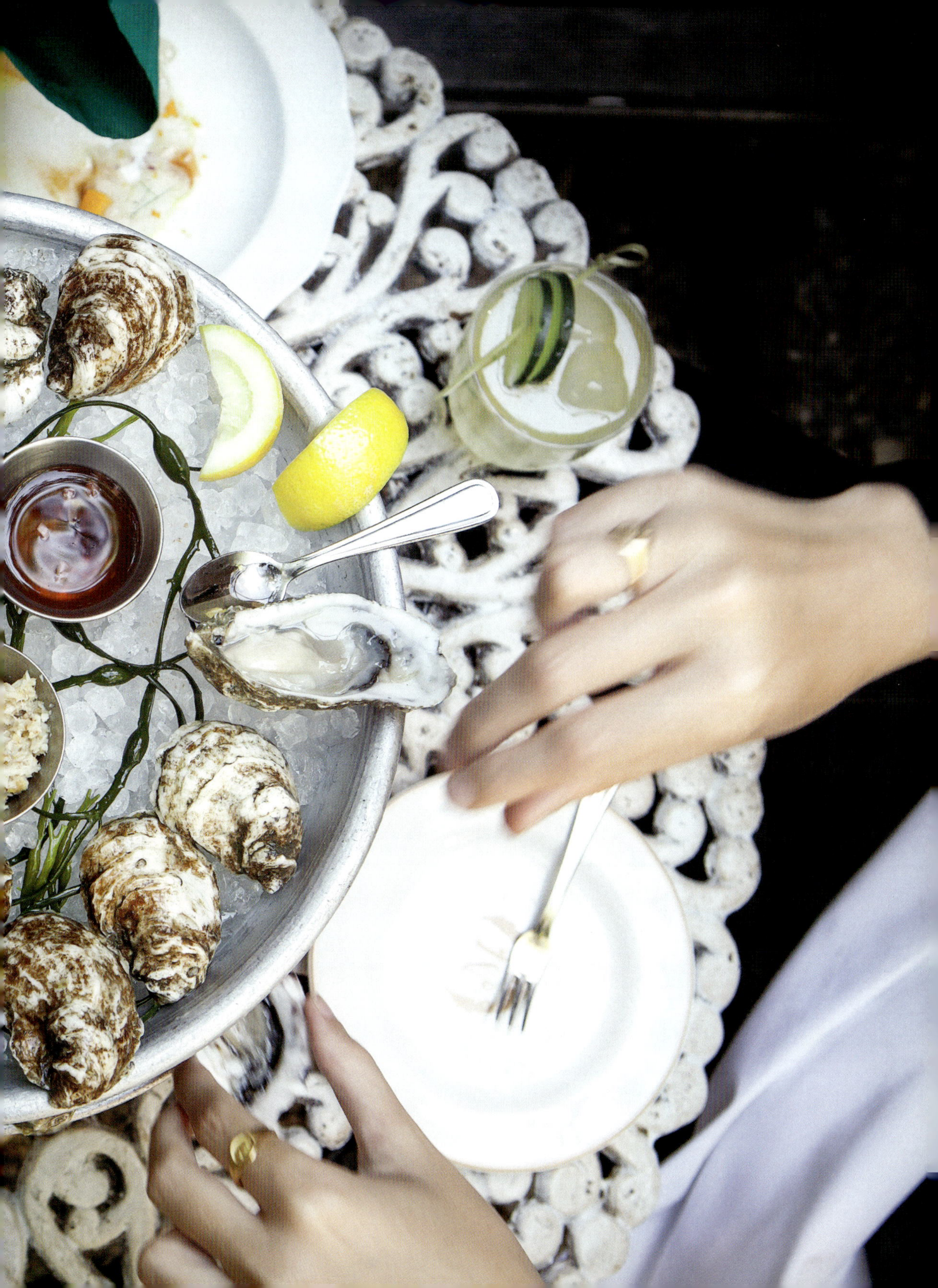

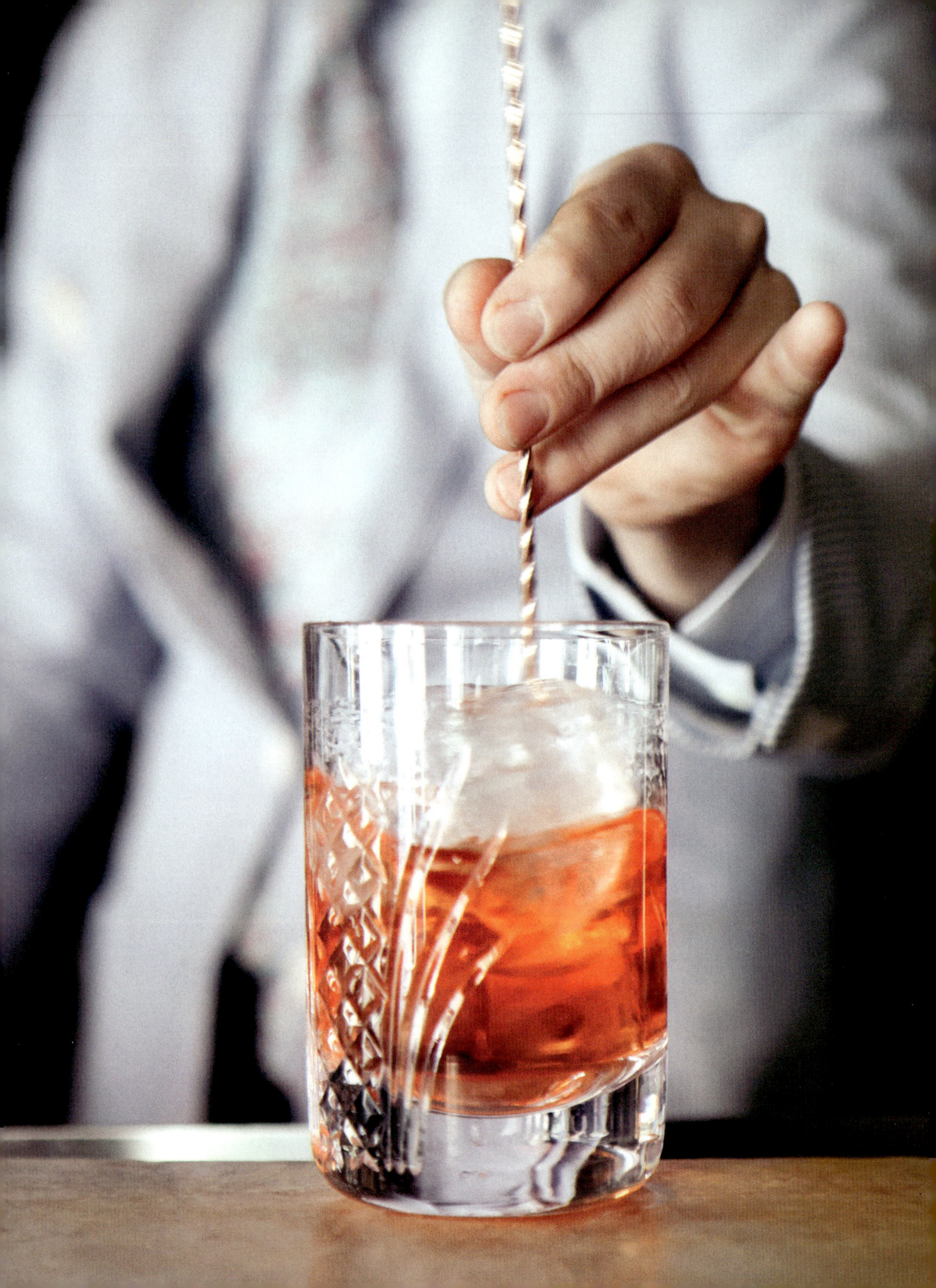

APERITIF

**THE LOW-PROOF
COCKTAIL MOVEMENT** 68

RULES OF THE APERITIF COCKTAIL 75

APERITIF HOUR IN AMERICA 82

APERITIF AT HOME 93

RECETTES

Rivington Punch 63 ◆ *C Vidal* 64 ◆ *Lysette* 70
A Scented Stretch 73 ◆ *Al Fresco Spritz* 78
Qui Oui? 81 ◆ *The Shining Path* 85 ◆ *Gentlemen Caller* 86
The St-Germain *Cocktail* 90 ◆ *Tête-à-Tête* 95

IN THE UNITED STATES, *HAPPY HOUR* IS A LOADED PHRASE.

ON ITS FACE, IT'S a positive proposition—the tie-loosening, heels-ditching reprieve from a day at the office, aided by deep-discount drinks. But there's a negative connotation there, too. Mixing cheap booze and pent-up stress often translates to a night that ends way too early, or a casual gathering that morphs into an embarrassing morning-after story.

So how should we go about splitting the difference, capturing all the best aspects of this post-work practice without any of the pitfalls? Do as the Europeans do, of course.

Derived from the Latin *aperire*, meaning "to open," the aperitif is a centuries-old tradition steeped in simple elegance. Commonly consumed in France, Italy, and throughout the Mediterranean, aperitifs—from Italy's spritz to Spain's vermouth and soda—are thirst-quenching, low-alcohol beverages sipped socially to stimulate, or "open," one's appetite ahead of eating. But the aperitif's appeal is much broader than that. Many American bartenders, enamored with the versatility of the category, are doing their part to evangelize, tamping down the high-octane proclivities of US drinkers by introducing aperitifs—and their accompanying culture—to a new audience.

Often served with a light spread of snacks, aperitifs are consumed in an informal setting—a bar or restaurant, a public gathering space, or someone's home—around the same time a conventional happy hour would kick off. But the practice's importance extends far beyond readying one's stomach for a meal. "L'apéritif is more than a drink before a meal," writes Georgeanne Brennan in her book *Aperitif: Recipes for Simple Pleasures in the French Style*. "It is a national custom that, by deliberately setting apart time to share a drink and to socialize, engenders civility and conviviality."

In other words, the aperitif has long been ritualized, woven into the routine in such a way that it's become a vital facet of everyday life. And while many European countries embrace the tradition of a light, late-afternoon or early-evening cocktail gathering, the French have a particular affinity for the practice. Take it from the Parisian essayist Paul Morand: *"L'apéritif, c'est la prière du soir des Français"*—for the French, the aperitif is the evening prayer.

"An aperitif in France is not just a drink—it's part of our culture," says *St-Germain* global ambassador Camille Ralph Vidal, who grew up in the South of France. She embraced the custom early on, enjoying grenadine in her family's garden as her father drank pastis and her mother sipped wine. "There was no TV in the background, no video games, mobiles, or anything—just us sharing a moment together," she says. The term *aperitif*, in Vidal's eyes, refers to both a style of beverage and an overarching approach to life. "It's about making time to relax, unwind, enjoy, and appreciate things," she says.

Though the interpersonal value of the aperitif is an easy concept to grasp, defining what drinks actually fit the mold is a trickier task. "Aperitif can mean a lot of different things, which is what's cool about it," says bartender Alex Day, who is behind a number of the country's best cocktail bars. "It doesn't lock you into any frame or structure."

An aperitif should be low alcohol by volume, but besides that, there aren't too many hard-and-fast rules in place. There are, however, a few common characteristics. "They're supposed to be dry, to get your palate salivating," says bartender and drinks writer Naren Young. "Nothing too sweet, alcoholic, or heavy. It should be invigorating."

Fortified wines and various floral and herbal liqueurs, poured on the rocks or made into a simple cocktail, like a spritz, are common aperitifs, but the category is in no way limited to such options. "Champagne, a glass of white wine, or a crisp beer can be an aperitif," adds Young, who's built an extensive list at New York's Dante. "All these serve the same purpose."

Not only is the aperitif an important cultural ritual—a moment in the day that asks nothing except that you let your hair down—it's also a perspective on drinking that places "sessionability" above all else. The easy-drinking nature of a properly made aperitif leads to a natural propensity for multiple rounds, extending the precious time you spend with family and friends. "If the happy hour celebrates the end of the day, the aperitif celebrates the beginning of the night," says Vidal.

That doesn't mean sacrificing intrigue: "More than anything else, it just needs to have a good amount of complexity," says Atlanta bartender Greg Best of a successful aperitif. To achieve such results, Best and his contemporaries have developed a series of "pace car cocktails" they call suppressors. The low-alcohol yin to the Corpse Reviver family's revved-up yang, suppressors appear, in thirty to forty different forms, at cocktail bars around the country, from Best's Ticonderoga Club in Atlanta to California and back.

"Imbibing in this way gives you more staying power and a chance to keep a clear head," says Franky Marshall of Brooklyn's Le Boudoir, a Francophile who enjoys turning the uninitiated on to her many aperitif options.

Marshall's not alone in her mission to spread the aperitif gospel to guests accustomed to drinking in one lane. At New York's Nitecap, co-owned by Alex Day and Natasha David, the typical happy hour is swapped out for "aperitif hour," featuring discounted prices on that entire section of the extensive menu.

"When people think of that time of day, it's cheap beer, two-for-ones," says David, who says texture, achieved through additions like sherries and housemade syrups, is vital to a good aperitif. "I very much appreciate the European sense of drinking."

While these bartenders put much effort into promoting the concept of the aperitif to their customers, many also emphasize that it's not a topic that needs to be overanalyzed to be sincerely appreciated. "It's not something that's really fussed over that much," says Day. "It's meant to be thrown together, hanging out outdoors on a deck, finishing up a long day."

The more people familiarize themselves with the ease and appeal of the aperitif and its power to transport, the more this ritual will sneak into the collective American drinking consciousness—and stay there. "I don't really see it as a trend," says Young. "It's something that's going to keep going forever."

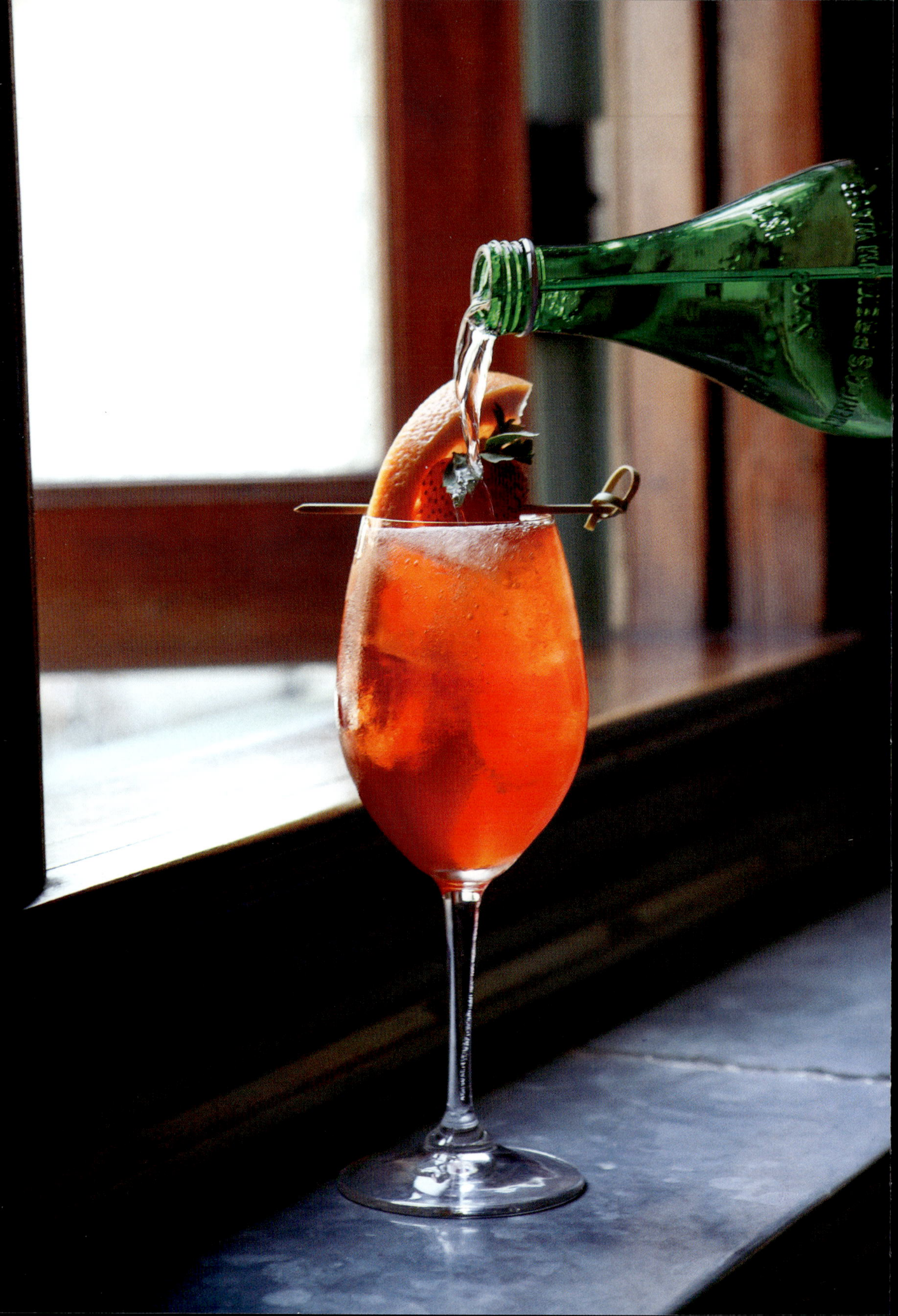

SERVES 1

Natasha David
—
Nitecap

RIVINGTON
PUNCH

THE RIVINGTON PUNCH MARRIES two of the most classic spritzes—the white wine spritzer and the Aperol Spritz—and then dresses them up in bright pink. A base of rosé combines with bittersweet Aperol, *St-Germain*, and raspberry liqueur for a fruit-forward fuchsia bubbler. And, of course, no punch or spritz would be complete without a fistful of fruit—in this case, a knockout one-two combination of grapefruit and strawberry.

2 ounces **dry rosé wine**
½ ounce **St-Germain**
1½ ounces **Aperol**
¼ ounce **raspberry liqueur, preferably Combier Framboise**
1 ounce **soda water**

GLASS

GARNISH Strawberry slices and grapefruit crescent

METHOD Stir all of the ingredients in a wine glass over ice. Garnish with strawberry slices and a grapefruit crescent.

APERITIF ◆ 63

SERVES 1

Pamela Wiznitzer
—
Seamstress

C VIDAL

"**I GRABBED THE *ST-GERMAIN*** and added some to the recipe," explains Pamela Wiznitzer of the trial-and-error process behind her tiki-inspired aperitif, "and it was the glue that brought it all together." Built on an amaro base, her C Vidal incorporates tropical elements like pineapple and lime, bridging the gap between the classic aperitif and the bolder canon of tiki drinks. To honor the missing ingredient that ultimately makes the drink pop, Wiznitzer named the cocktail after *St-Germain* brand ambassador Camille Ralph Vidal.

1½ ounces **Amaro Montenegro**
¾ ounce **St-Germain**
¼ ounce **vanilla syrup, preferably Giffard**
1 ounce **Madeira**
1 ounce **pineapple juice**
¾ ounce **lime juice**

GLASS

GARNISH Pineapple leaf

METHOD Shake all of the ingredients and strain into a highball glass over ice. Garnish with the pineapple leaf.

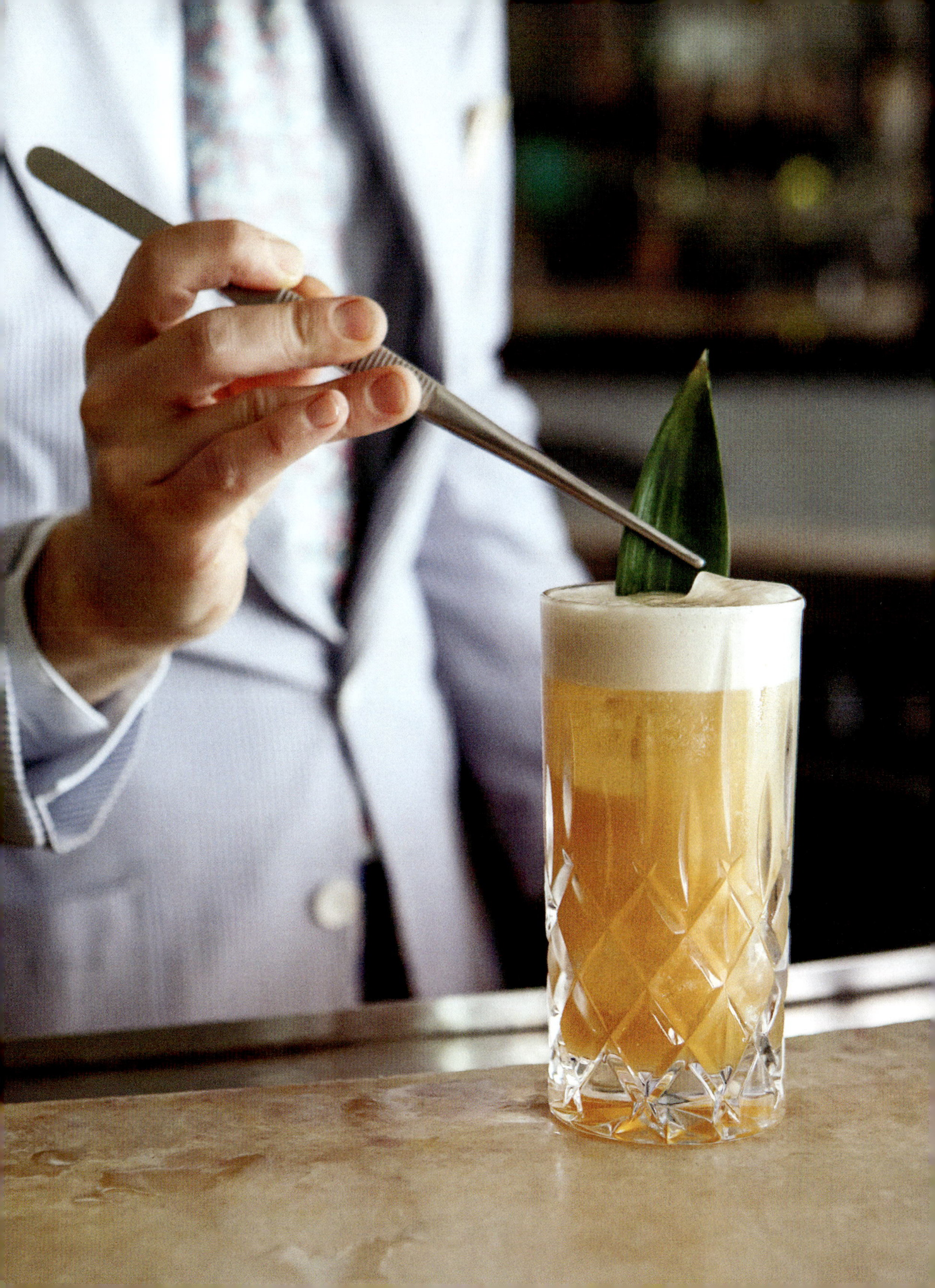

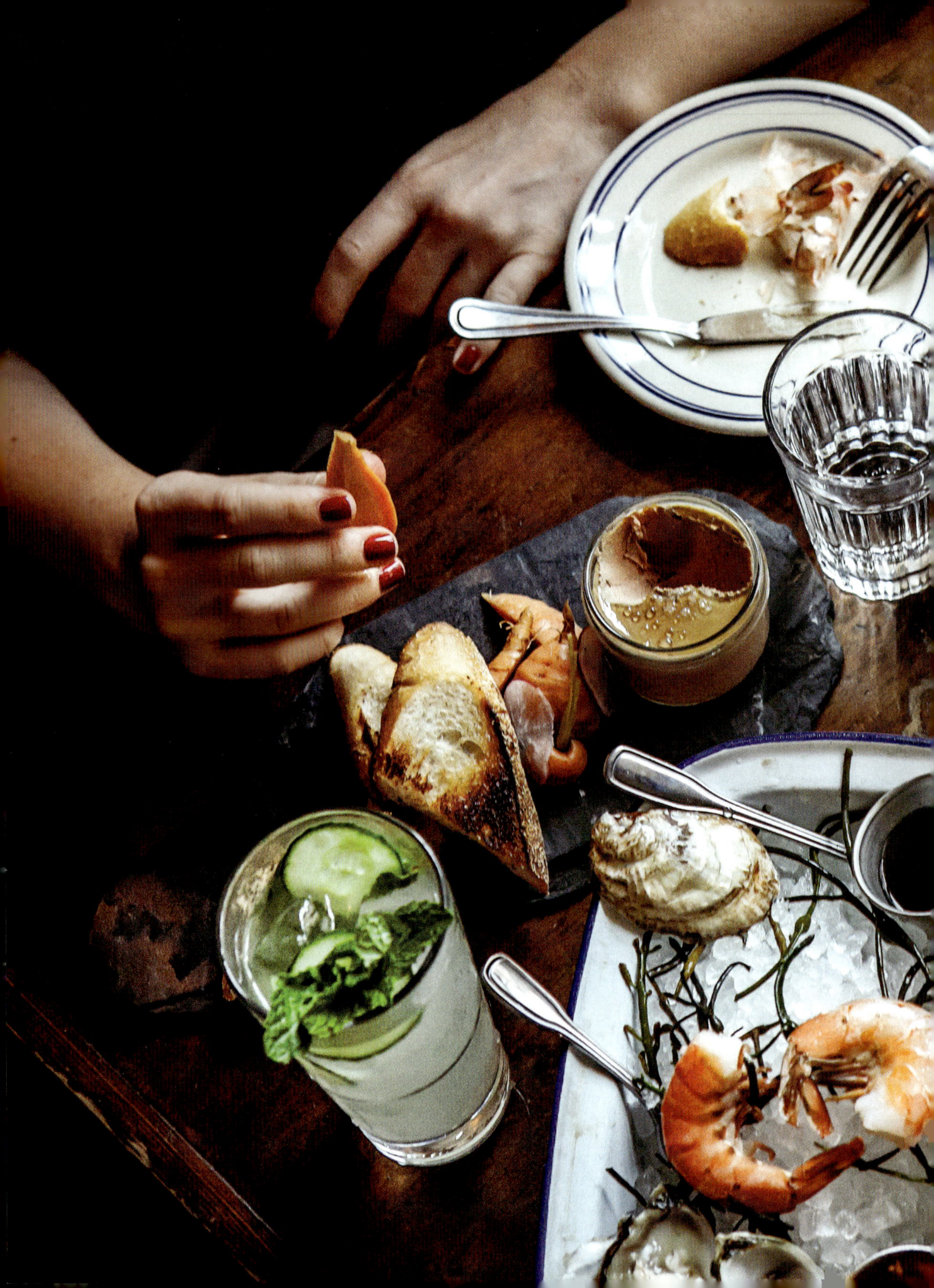

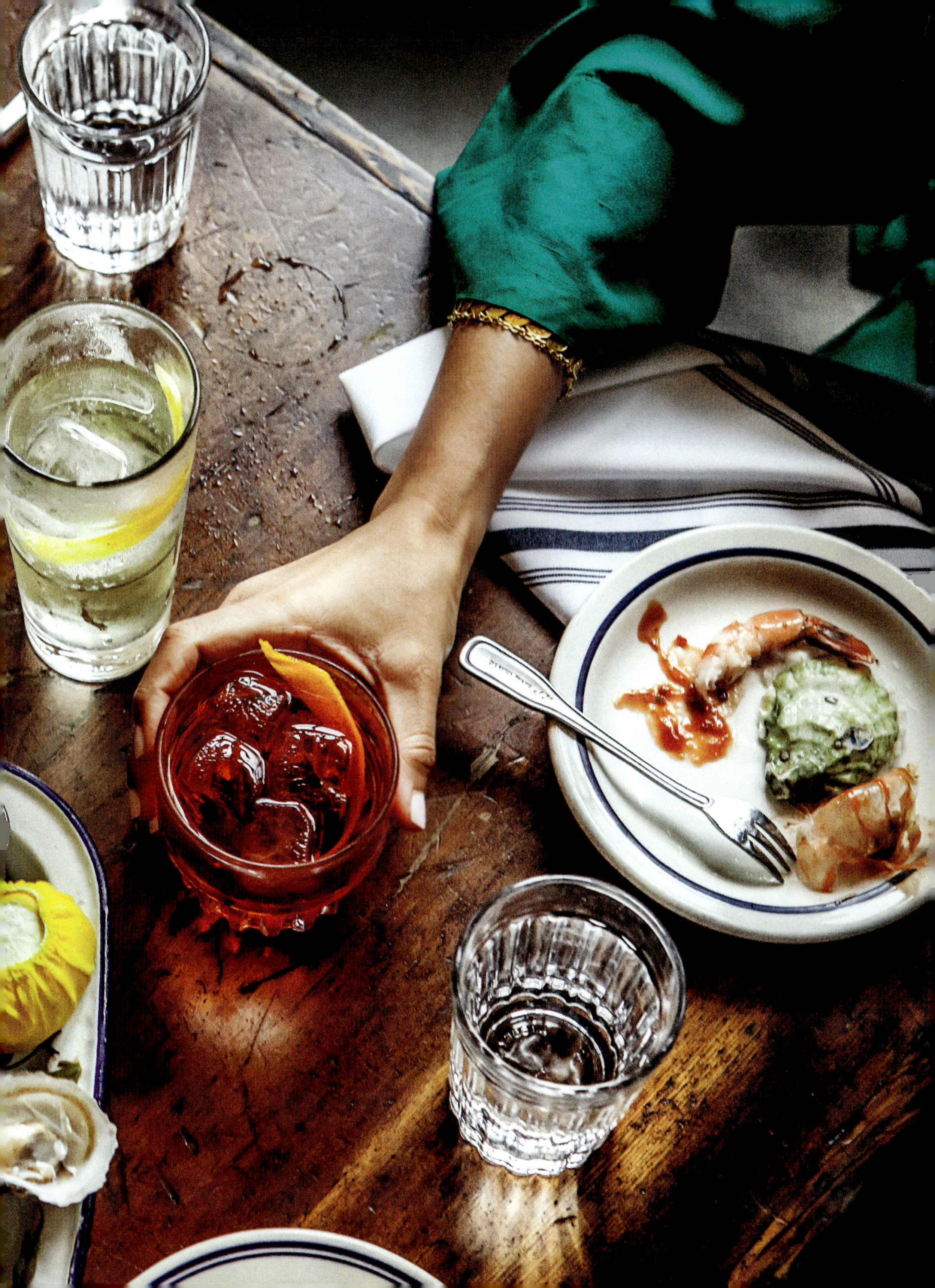

THE LOW-PROOF COCKTAIL MOVEMENT

The aperitif category has become a strong source of professional stimulation for bartenders, who relish the opportunity to play with subtler and more versatile flavors. "On a creative level, aperitifs and low-alcohol cocktails present a new format for us to play with," says bar owner Alex Day. "You can strip away the strong personality of a high-proof spirit and begin exploring flavors in different ways. It's a whole new avenue for creating cocktails."

In many ways, this movement mirrors comparable trends in the craft beer and wine spheres, which have begun steering away from over-the-top, shock-and-awe experimentation in favor of nuance. A renaissance of once-forgotten ingredients has run in tandem with this change.

The low-ABV (alcohol by volume) movement extends all the way from brunch to the nightcap, and from spritzes to stirred cocktails. Such growth has not only manifested itself in a full spectrum of lo-fi, creative cocktails but in well-informed bar guests who are now familiar with a wider range of ingredients. "The consumer base is just far more up-to-date, far more savvy," says Atlanta-based Greg Best, who peddles a variety of popular low-ABV cocktails at his Ticonderoga Club. But there's still plenty of work to be done in softening the hold that higher-proof cocktails once had on the American cocktail drinker. "What we try to do is help bridge the gap—to say, 'Drinking this way isn't embarrassing.' You can enjoy yourself without jumping headlong into it."

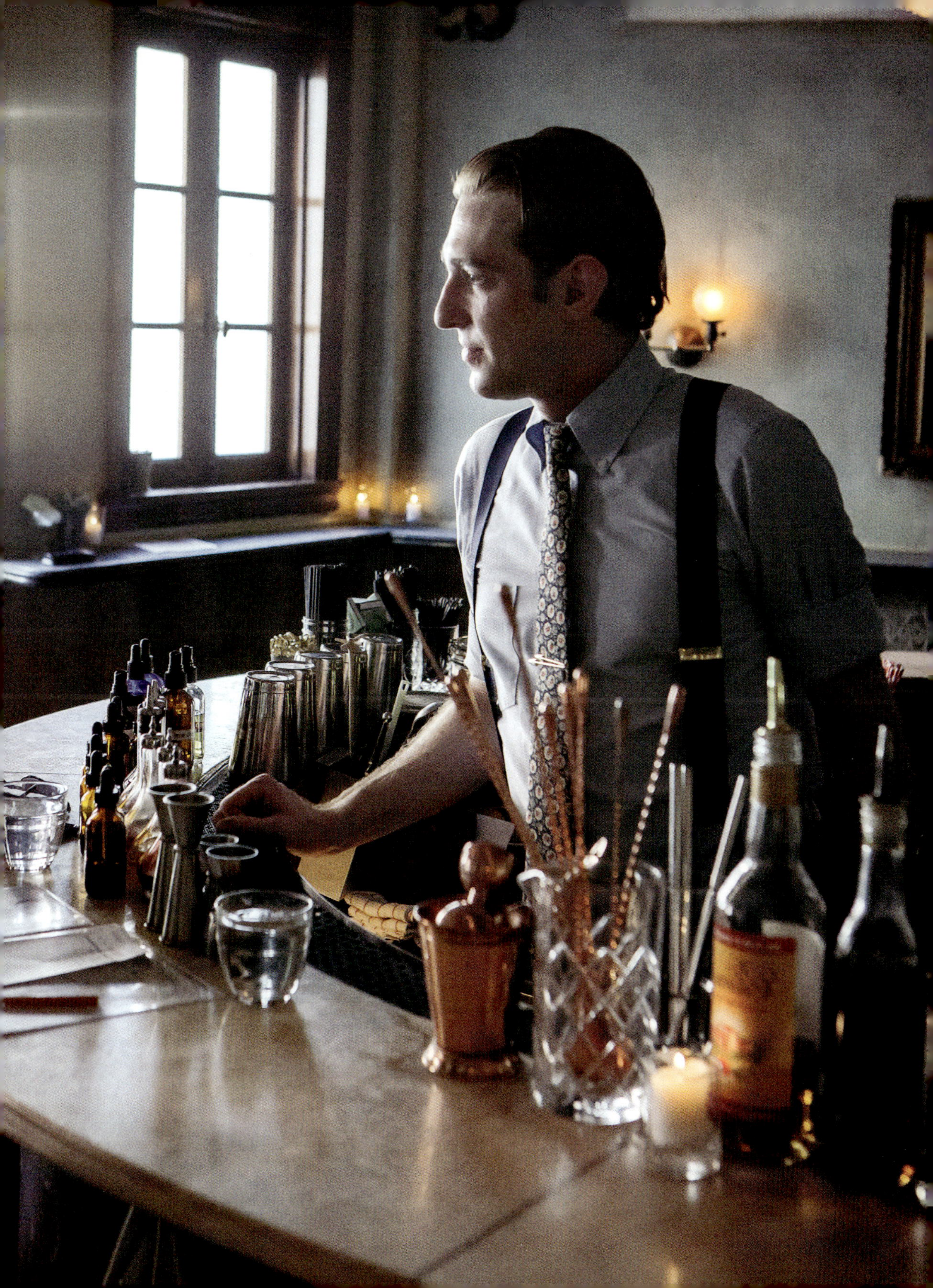

SERVES 1

Franky Marshall
—
Le Boudoir

LYSETTE

THE HALLMARKS OF THE aperitif—are the driving forces behind the Lysette, a three-ingredient cocktail as relevant for the home bartender as it is for the pro. "After all," explains bartender Franky Marshall, "the less time you spend making drinks, the more time you have to enjoy good company." In a nod to the aperitif's origins, the components are all French—from the gentle bitterness of Salers to the light, floral notes of *St-Germain* to the fizzy smack of Kronenbourg.

¾ ounce **St-Germain**
¾ ounce **Salers gentian liqueur**
1 ounce **lager, preferably Kronenbourg 1664**

GLASS

GARNISH Grapefruit peel, 2 chrysanthemum blossoms (or other edible flowers)

METHOD Combine the *St-Germain* and gentian liqueur in an ice-filled stemmed glass or goblet. Stir briefly. Top with the lager. Stir once to integrate. Express the grapefruit peel, then discard. Garnish with chrysanthemum blossoms.

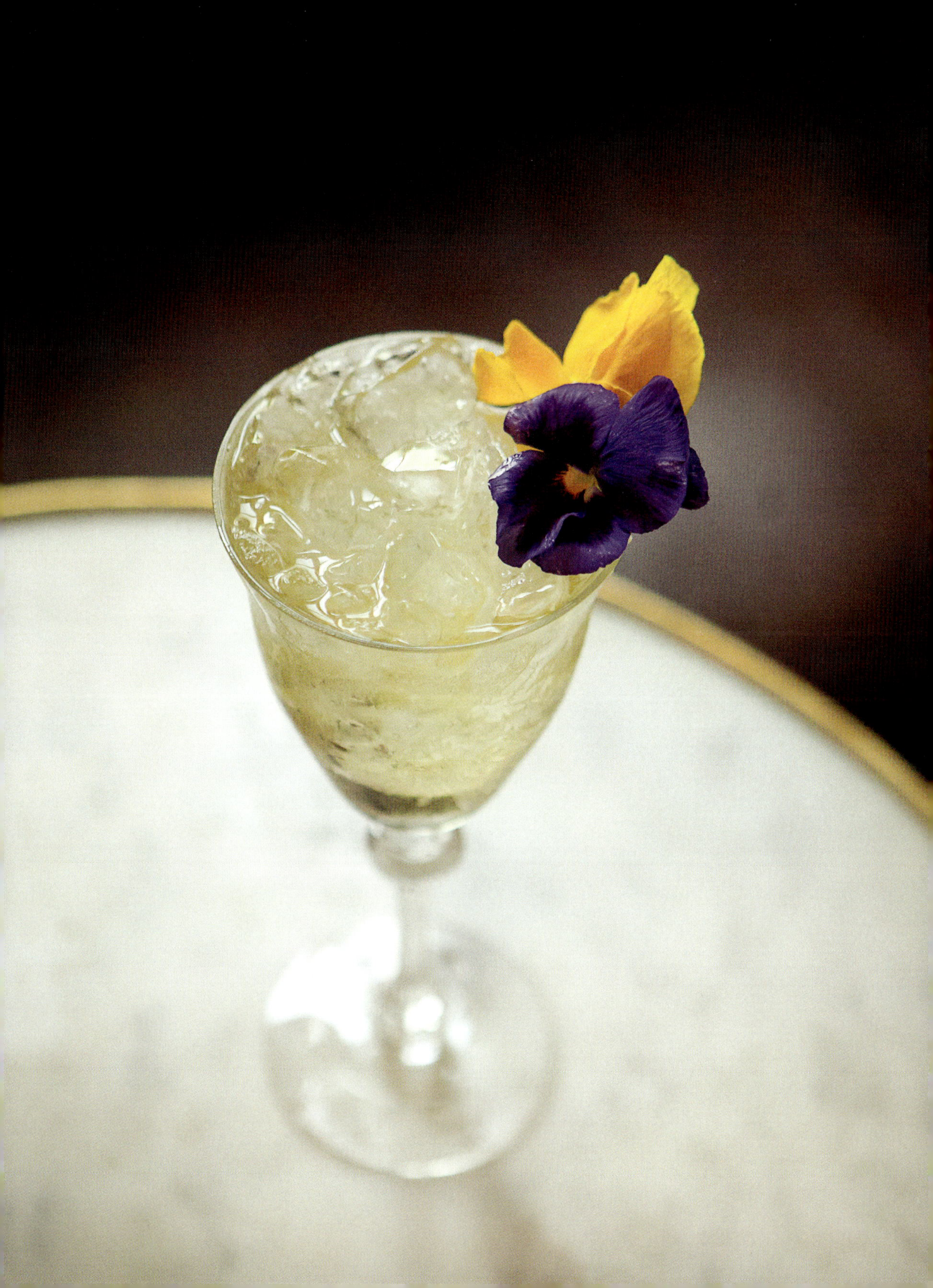

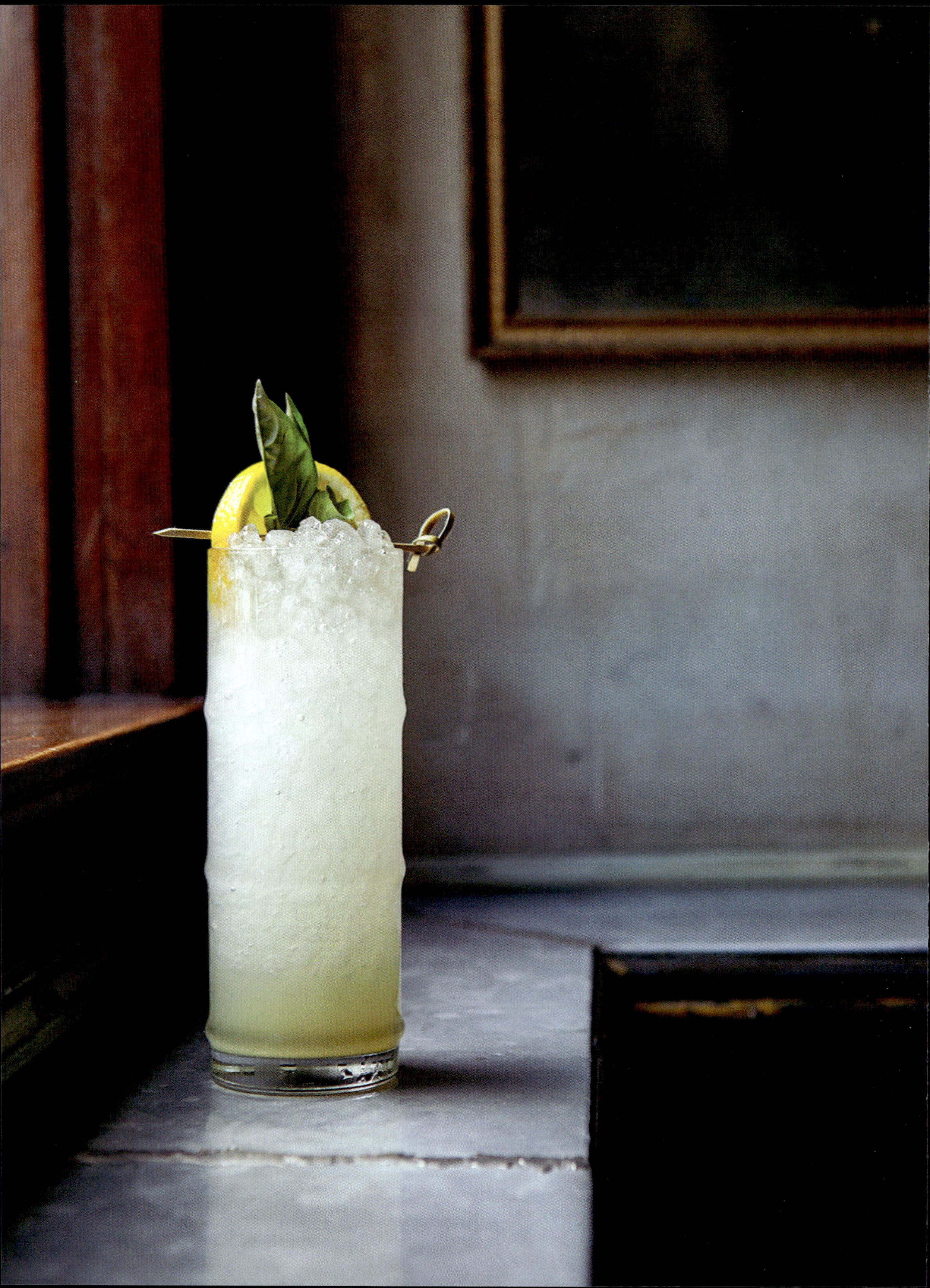

SERVES
1

Greg Best
—
Ticonderoga Club

A SCENTED
STRETCH

"MORE THAN ANYTHING else, it just needs to have a good amount of complexity," says bartender Greg Best of a successful aperitif. Best and his contemporaries boast impressive credentials for creating such recipes, having developed a series of highly compelling, low-alcohol drinks for Atlanta's Ticonderoga Club. A Scented Stretch is one such drink. Built on a base of white rum, it gets its sweetness from honey syrup and *St-Germain,* and its acidity from lemon juice and a shot of crisp white wine. A splash of soda water and an aromatic sprig of Thai basil lengthen the cocktail without sacrificing flavor, making the drink a steady, low-proof "pace car cocktail" to keep your night cruising.

1 ounce **Holland style white rum**
¾ ounce **strained lemon juice**
½ ounce **St-Germain**
½ ounce **crisp white wine, preferably grüner veltliner or Sancerre**
¼ ounce **honey syrup (3:1, honey:water)**
1 ounce **soda water**

GLASS

GARNISH Pinch of flaky salt, such as Maldon, lemon wheel, small sprig of Thai basil

METHOD Combine all of the ingredients except the soda water in a Collins glass over crushed ice. Add the soda water and stir gently. Garnish with the salt, lemon wheel, and Thai basil.

APERITIF ◆ 73

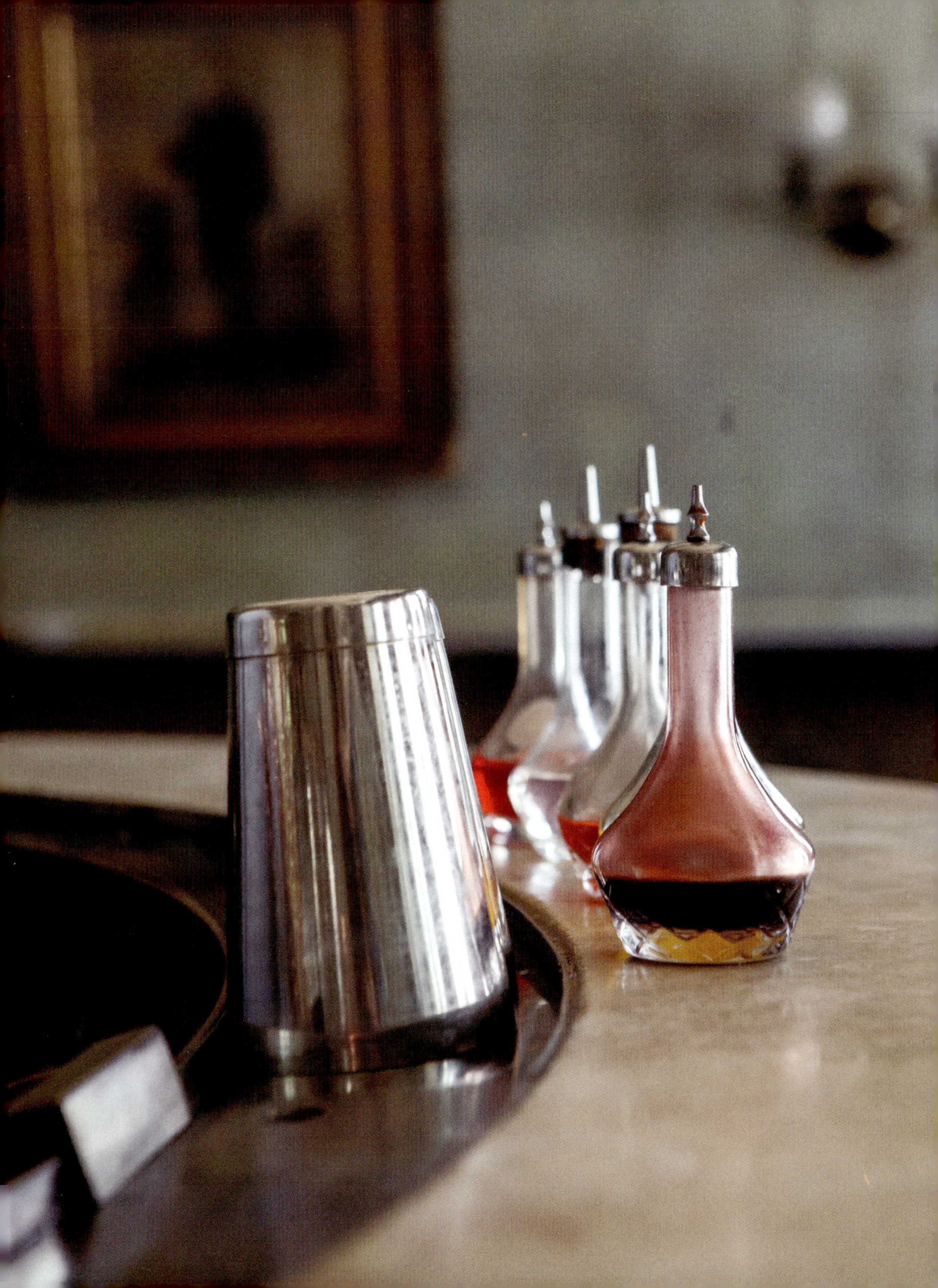

RULES OF
THE APERITIF COCKTAIL

- **GET LOW.** In addition to being a social draw, the utilitarian function of an aperitif is to get you ready for dinner—not ruin it. The aperitif can be a lot of things—a mixed drink, a glass of sparkling wine, an ice-cold beer—but there is one unifying feature: sessionability. These are drinks that should be low enough in alcohol that they allow you to go the distance.

- **DON'T SWEAT THE DETAILS.** While all the drinks in this book offer exact measurements, the spirit of the aperitif in France, Italy, and beyond is one of malleability. A recipe can certainly be taken literally, but it can also be a source of inspiration. Think of each as a jumping-off point for your own creations.

- **GET OUTSIDE.** During the aperitif hour in Europe, many cities become urban living rooms with customers spilling out into the streets and squares. There's a reason: Aperitifs somehow just seem to taste better when sipped out in the sun.

- **SHARING IS CARING.** The beauty of aperitif culture is that it's as much about people as it is about drinks. Surround yourself with the ones you love when you're pouring—the rest should fall into place.

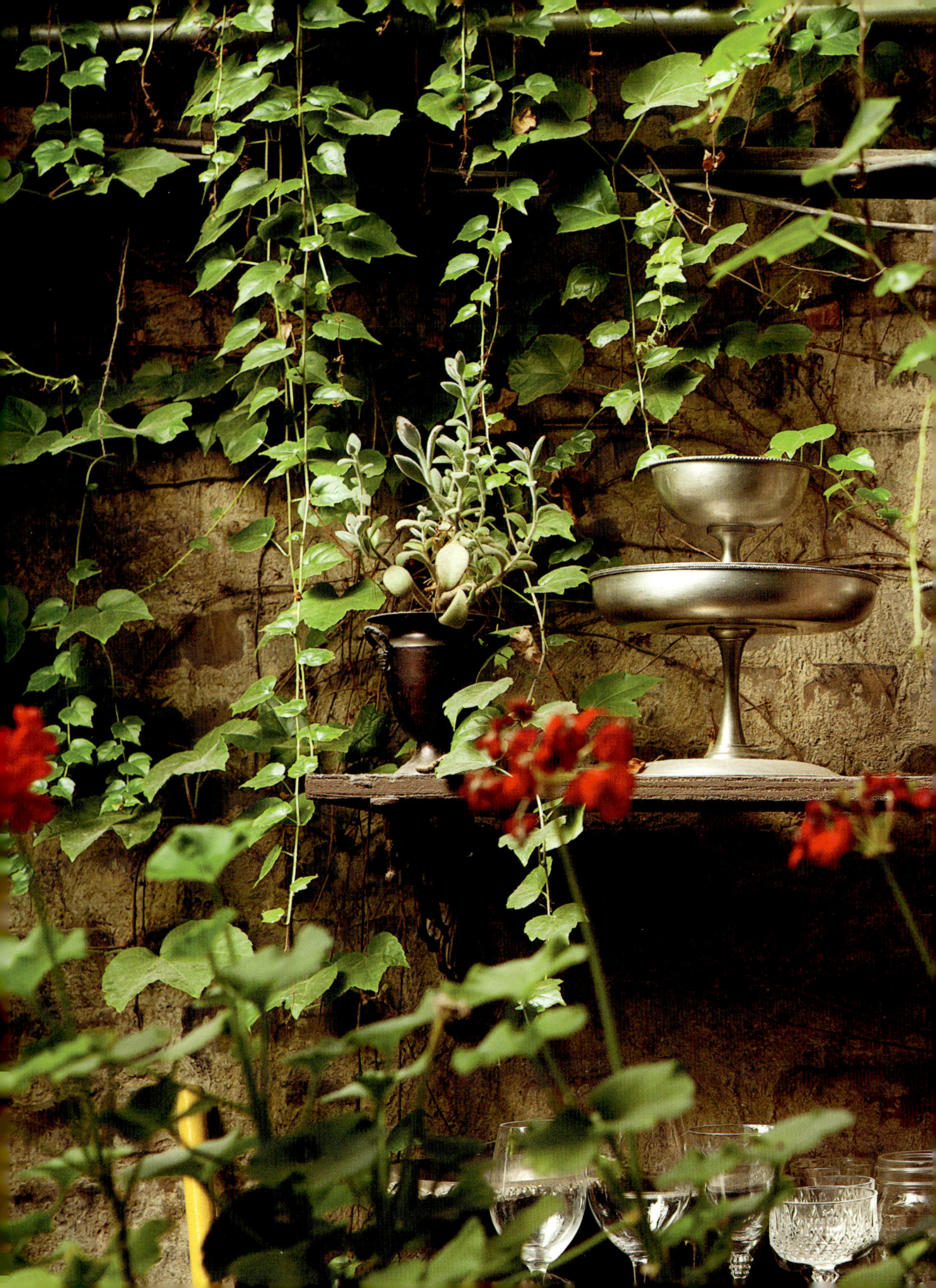

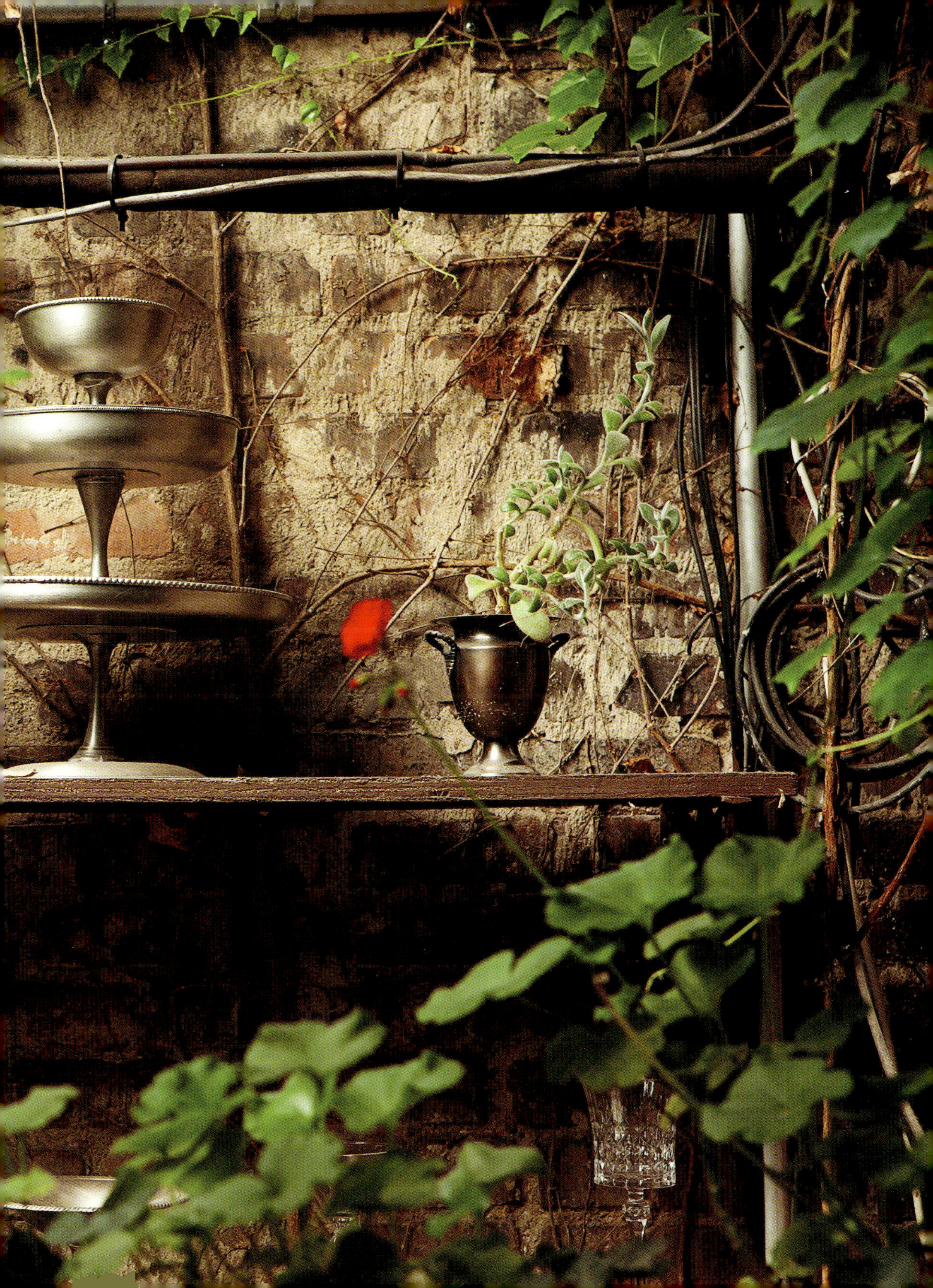

SERVES
1-4

Naren Young
—
Dante

AL FRESCO
SPRITZ

THOUGH THE APERITIF COMES in many forms, the Al Fresco Spritz keeps close to the classic interpretation—not too sweet, alcoholic, or heavy, and, most importantly, effervescent. Naren Young bumps up the botanicals with a measure of gin, which complements the floral notes of *St-Germain*, all balanced with a dose of acidity by way of lime. Young, a self-professed sucker for beautiful garnishes, elevates the drink with an impressive array of fruit, from green grapes to kiwi wheels to starfruit, which turns this batchable cocktail into a party unto itself. *Note: For a single serving, divide all of the ingredients by four.*

6 ounces **bianco vermouth, preferably Martini & Rossi®**
3 ounces **St-Germain**
2 ounces **London dry gin**
1 ounce **lime juice**
Sparkling water, preferably Perrier, to top
Prosecco, to top
2 to 4 **cucumber wheels**

GLASS

GARNISH 6 green grapes, 3 lime wheels, 3 kiwi wheels, 3 starfruit, 3 green apple slices, 3 cucumber slices

METHOD Combine the vermouth, *St-Germain*, gin, and lime juice in a pitcher over ice and stir. Top with equal parts Perrier and prosecco. To serve, place a cucumber wheel in each glass and pour in the spritz.

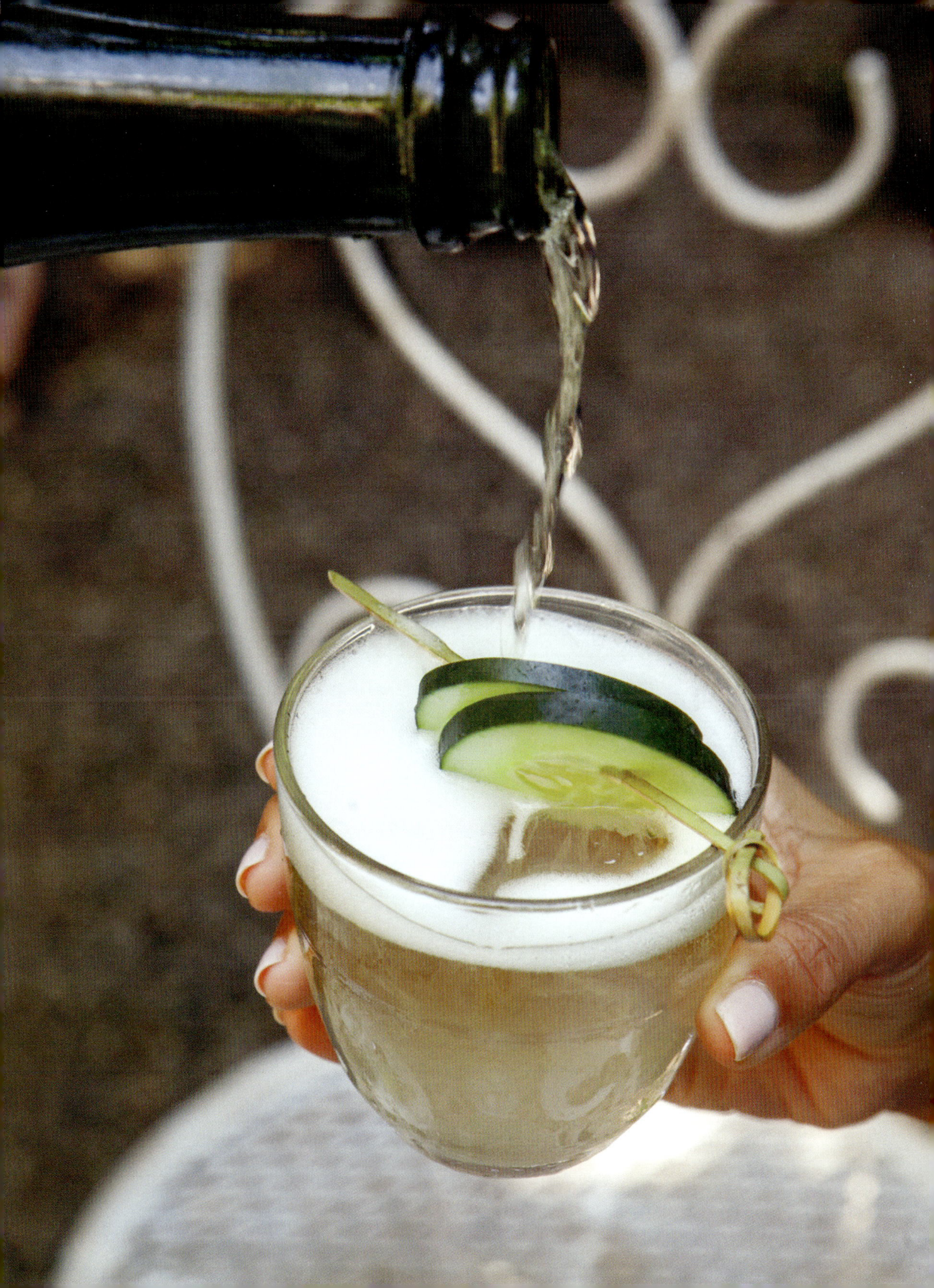

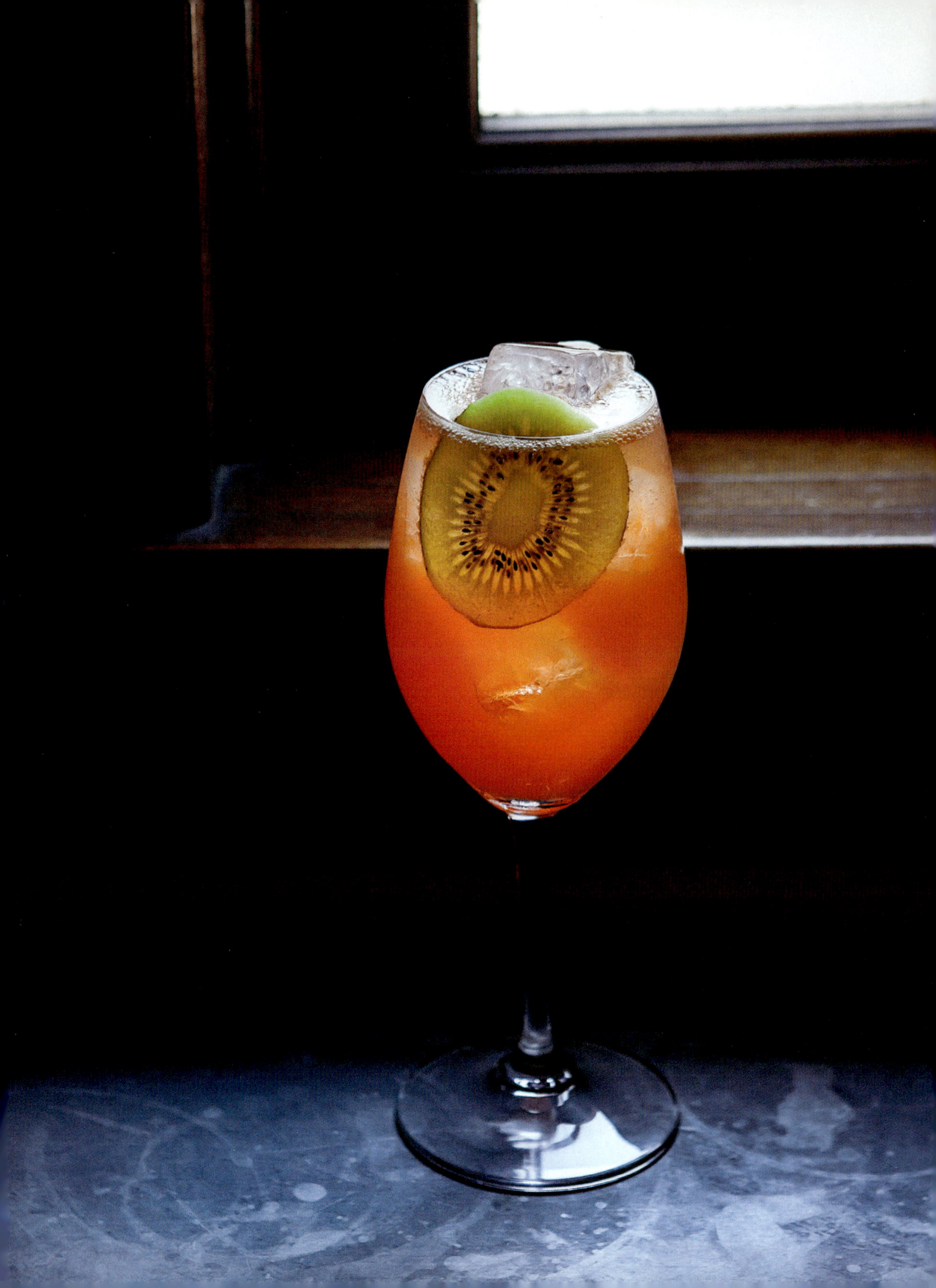

SERVES
1

Nico de Soto
—
Mace

QUI OUI?

A TWIST ON A twist, Nico de Soto's Qui Oui? plays off an Aperol Spritz rendition created for his Parisian restaurant Daroco. Where his original recipe included the addition of aquavit, Qui Oui? substitutes *St-Germain* for a more fruit-forward, floral profile. A play on words, *"qui oui?"* ("yes who?") phonetically resembles "kiwi," the secret ingredient in this aperitif.

½ ounce **St-Germain**
1½ ounces **Aperol**
½ ounce **kiwi syrup (see page 152)**
¾ ounce **lemon juice**
Pinch of **Himalayan pink salt**
Prosecco, to top

GLASS

GARNISH Dehydrated kiwi slice or fresh kiwi slice

METHOD Shake all of the ingredients, except the prosecco, with ice. Strain into a wine glass with ice, top with prosecco, and garnish with the kiwi slice.

APERITIF ◆ 81

APERITIF HOUR
IN AMERICA

Though the aperitif is both linguistically and culturally native to Europe, the past several years have seen a gradual, but significant, uptick in the United States. In Seattle, Barnacle serves a seafood-centric menu complemented by a staggering Italian amari list. Alta Linea, in New York's High Line Hotel, can knock out classic spritzes just as skillfully as nouveau riffs like Frozen Negronis. Americano, in Portland, Oregon, has tapped into the sociable spirit of the aperitif, packing in a jovial crowd nightly.

Meanwhile, bartender Naren Young's drink menu at Dante brings the European aperitivo bar to New York's Greenwich Village. Young has witnessed this shift firsthand; he's had a front-row seat behind his bar as the aperitif has moved toward the mainstream. "It's not just a category of drinks—it's aperitif as a lifestyle," says Young, whose Negroni Sessions happy hour has lured drinkers interested in his daring variations on the classic. "It's much more civilized than the American style, which is, by and large, more of an aggressive drinking culture."

Since the aperitif is so deeply linked with a time of day, marketing the aperitif to an early-evening crowd is a logical move for on-board bartenders. At New York's Nitecap, aperitif hour, featuring discounts on low-octane, Euro-inspired drinks, has replaced the typical postwork drinking deals. "We're trying to articulate happy hour in a more adult way," says Alex Day, who is co-owner of Nitecap and five other bars around the country. He is sure, however, to draw an important distinction between this drinking style and the vague concept of "luxury." The aperitif, while elegant, is never high-minded or snobby.

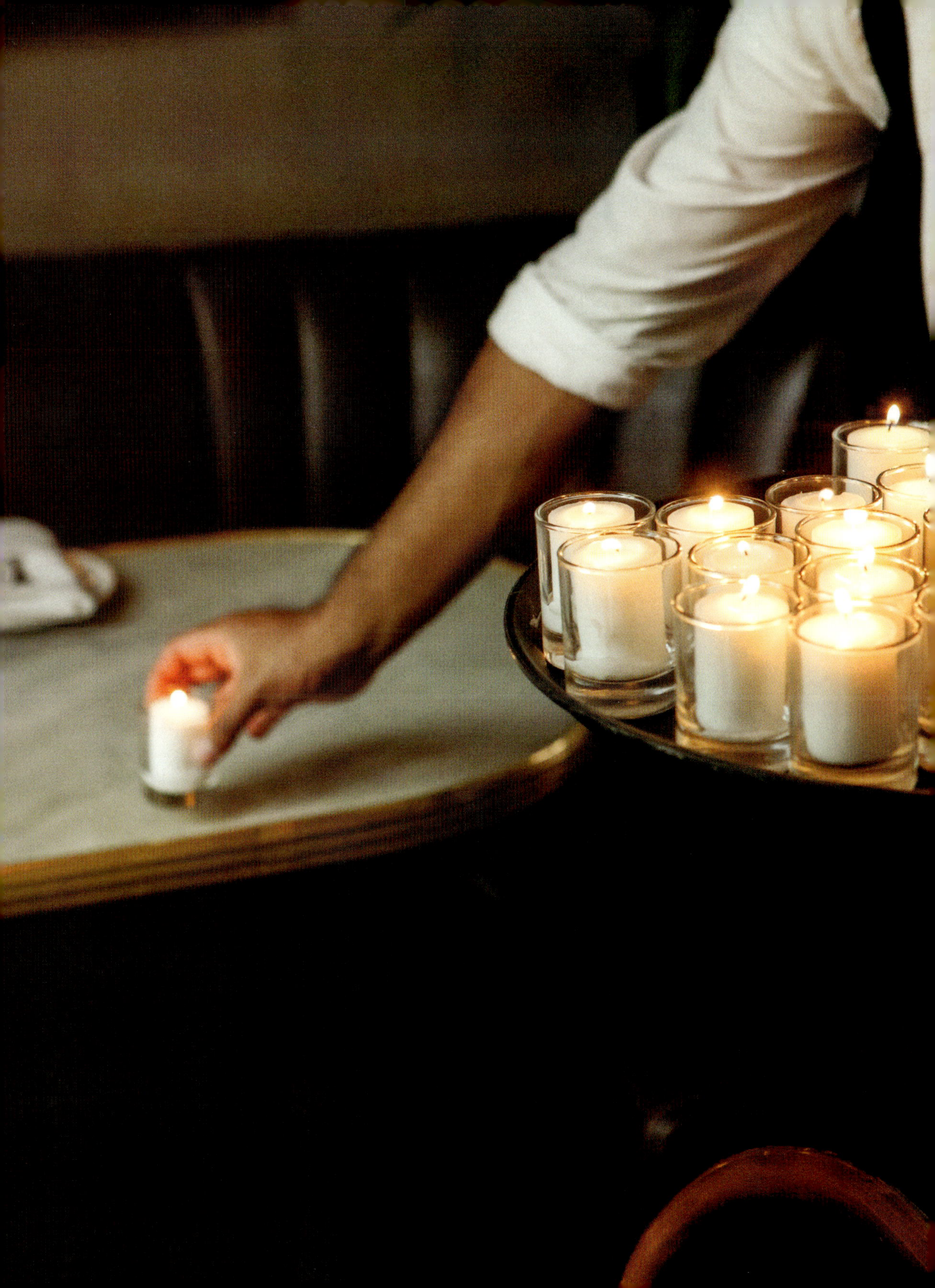

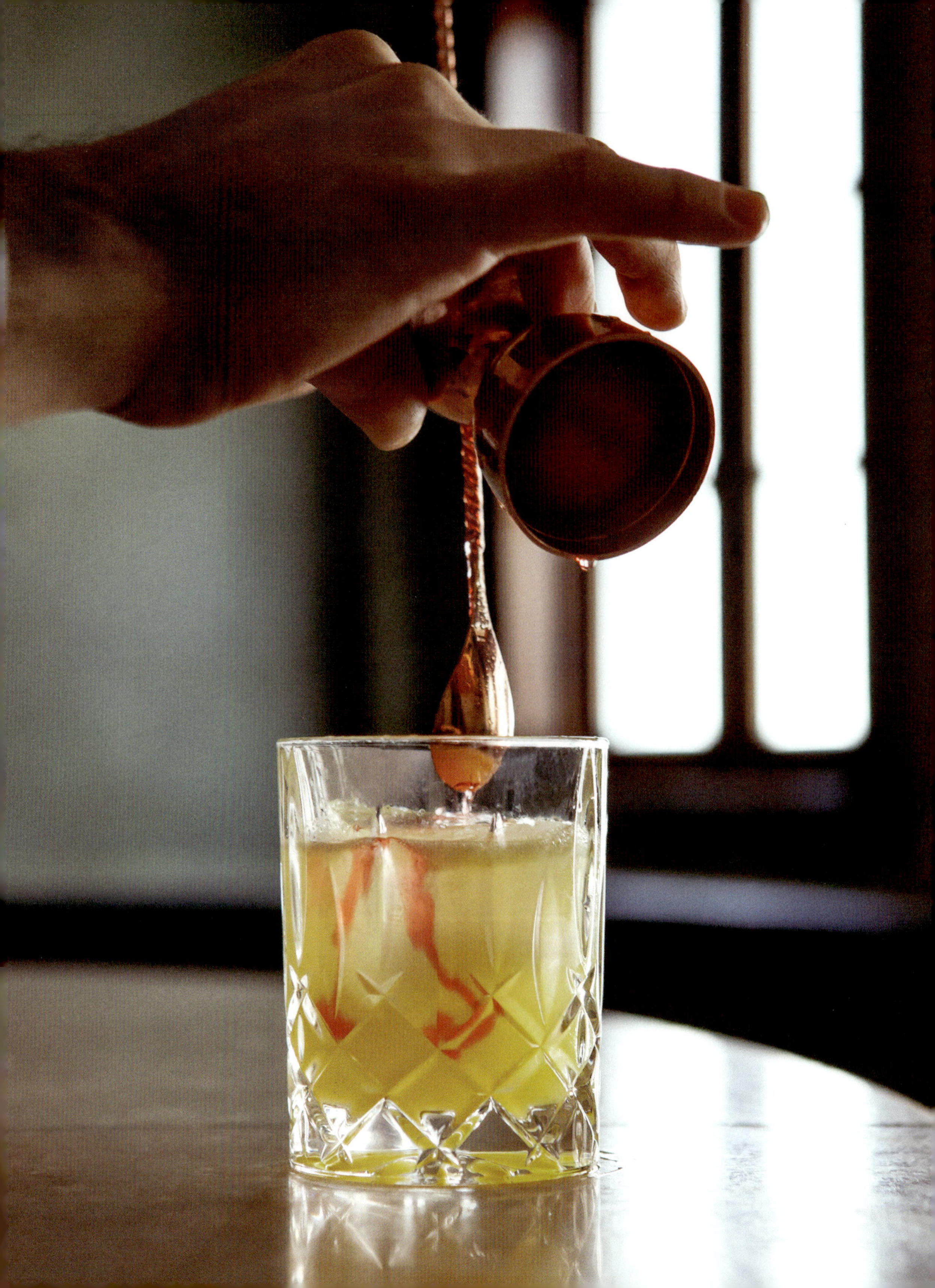

SERVES 1

Will Elliott

Maison Premiere

THE SHINING
PATH

FOR HIS BRACING PRE-DINNER drink, Will Elliott primes the palate with a double dose of gentian. "Gentian really gets the appetite raging," explains Elliott, who incorporates four French aperitifs—Salers, Avèze, *St-Germain* and Maurin Quina—into this classically bitter aperitif. *St-Germain* offers a counter to the bracing bitterness of Avèze, while the float of cherry-based Maurin Quina offers a hit of fruit on the nose and the palate.

¼ ounce **St-Germain**
½ ounce **lemon juice**
½ ounce **lemon cordial (see page 152)**
½ ounce **Avèze gentian liqueur**
¾ ounce **Salers gentian liqueur**
Maurin Quina, to top

GLASS

GARNISH Maurin Quina float

METHOD Combine all of the ingredients in a shaking tin. Shake with ice and fine strain into a double rocks glass over a large cube. Top with a float of Maurin Quina.

APERITIF ◆ 85

SERVES 1

Abigail Gullo
—
Compère Lapin

GENTLEMAN CALLER

IN HER GENTLEMAN CALLER, Abigail Gullo relies on the botanicals of gin, the bitterness of Aperol, and the dryness and perceivable acidity of fino sherry to enhance the florality of *St-Germain*. In combination, these traditional aperitif flavors serve to brighten the palate, making it the perfect accompaniment to pre-dinner snacks.

1 ounce **London dry gin**
1 ounce **fino en rama sherry**
¾ ounce **St-Germain**
¾ ounce **Aperol**

GLASS

GARNISH Lemon peel

METHOD Stir all of the ingredients with ice and strain into a chilled Nick & Nora glass. Garnish with the lemon peel.

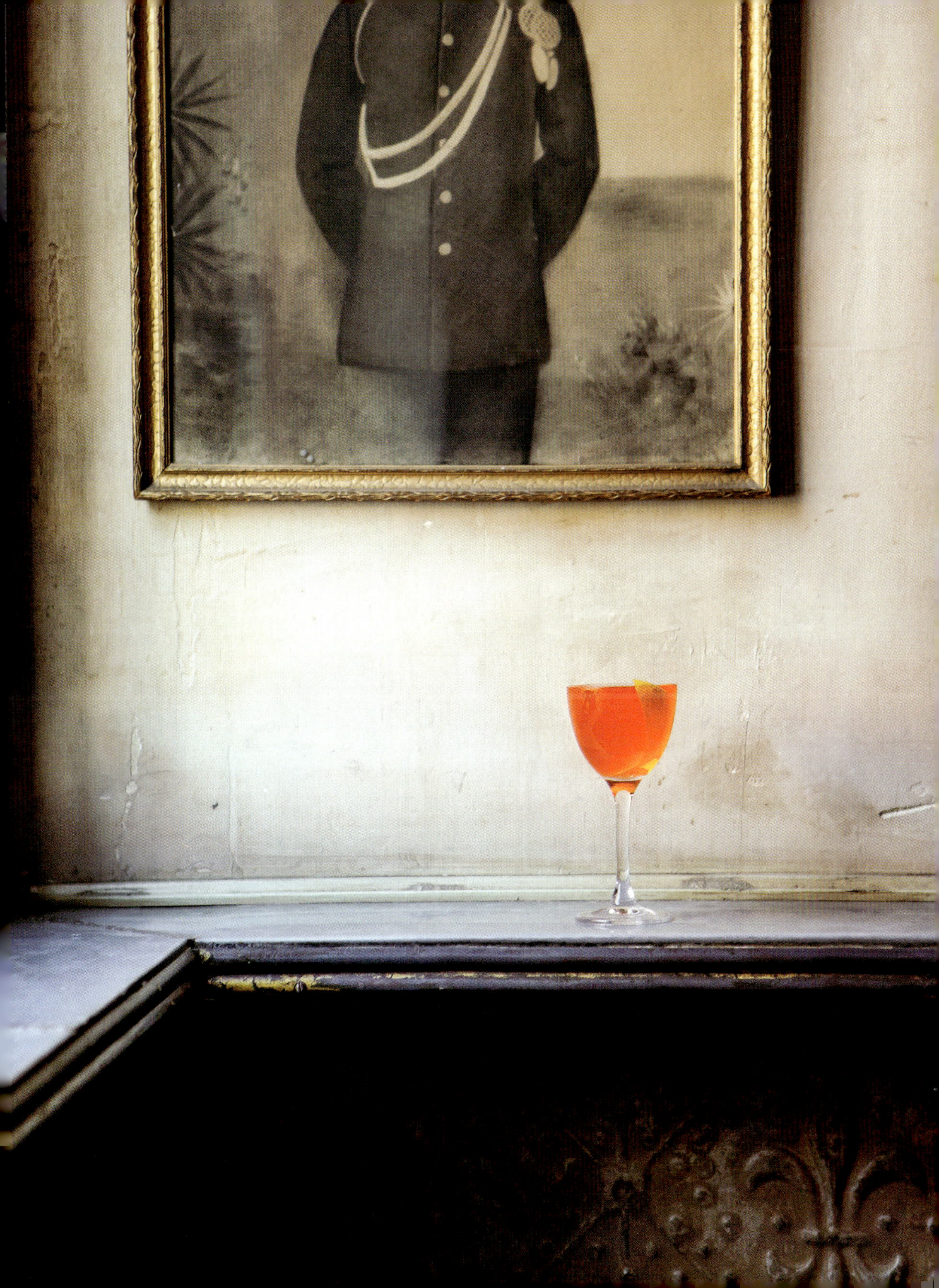

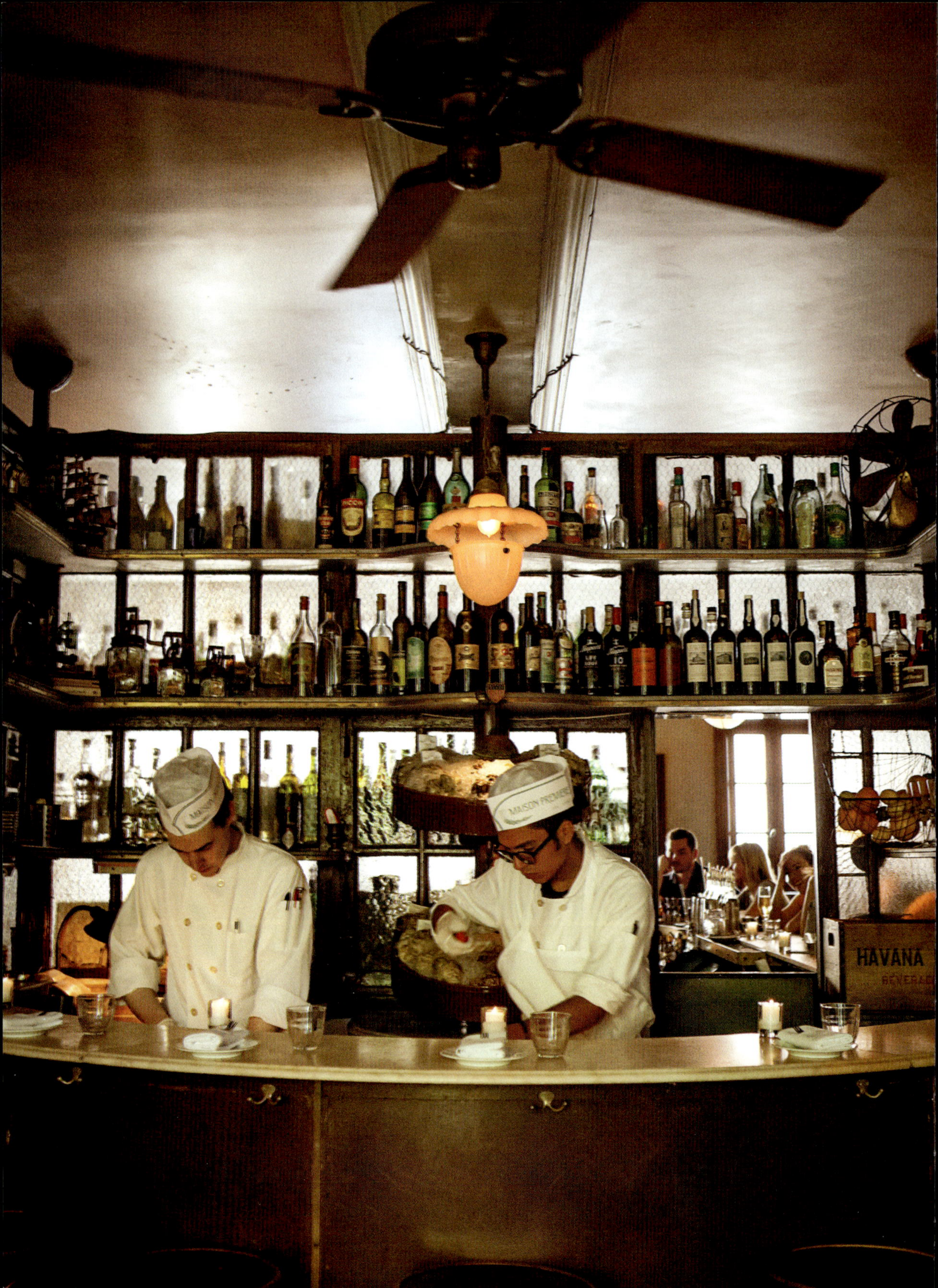
HAVANA

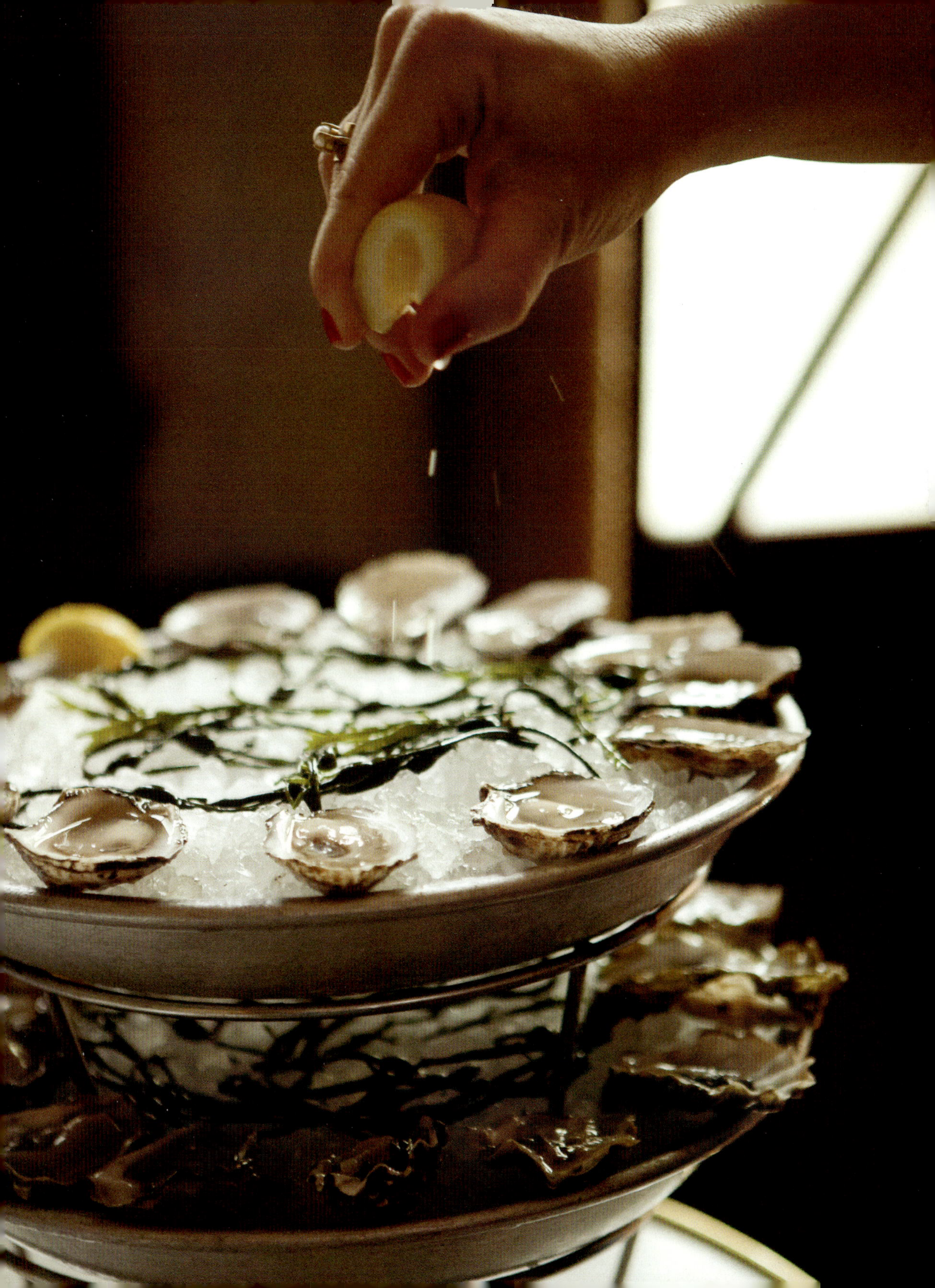

SERVES 1

Robert Cooper

THE ST-GERMAIN COCKTAIL

THE ST-GERMAIN COCKTAIL, the classic spritz variation fueled by the iconic elderflower liqueur, embodies the spirit of low-alcohol conviviality prevalent throughout Europe. Light, floral, and refreshing, it's a warm-weather go-to, easy in both execution and drinkability.

1½ ounces **St-Germain**
2 ounces **dry sparkling wine**
2 ounces **soda water**

GLASS

GARNISH Lemon twist

METHOD Combine all of the ingredients in a Collins glass over ice. Stir gently, and garnish with a lemon twist.

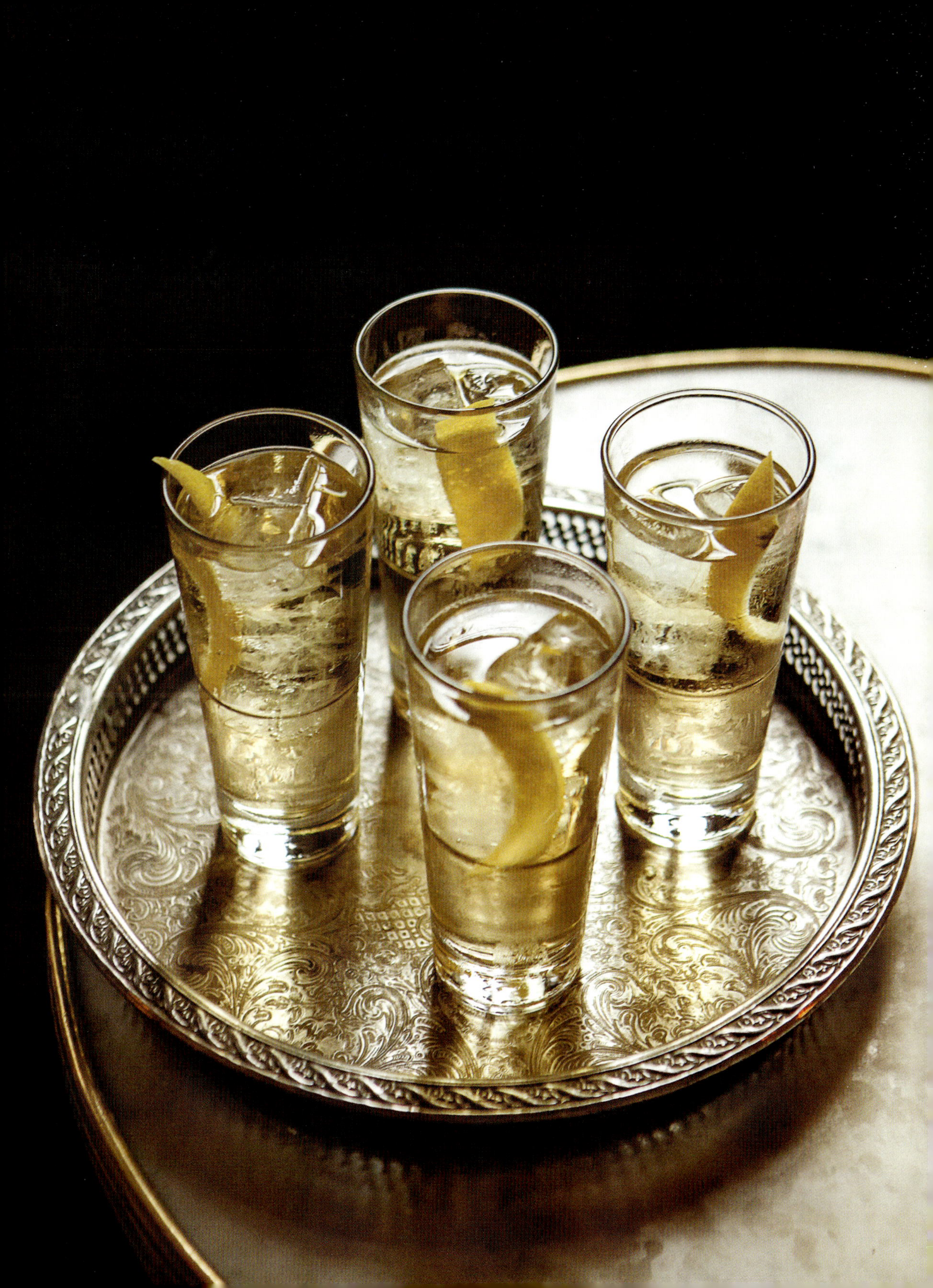

APERITIF
AT HOME

While the golden-hour plaza or bustling café have both become welcome accessories to the pre-dinner drink, in France the culture of the aperitif is as much a fixture of the home as it is an evening out. Transporting this ritual from bar to living room doesn't require much more than a few snacks and a modest home bar. Herewith, a few pro tips:

- **STOCK UP.** It takes very little to whip up a proper aperitif cocktail. Make sure you have a few select liqueurs on hand (think *St-Germain*, of course, plus bitter liqueurs, like Campari, and fruit liqueurs), a couple bottles of vermouth (blanc and rouge, preferably), some lighter spirits, like gin, several bottles of dry sparkling wine, and a small selection of citrus and fresh herbs.

- **KEEP THE BUBBLES HANDY.** The archetypal aperitif drink is meant to be forgiving. If the results aren't quite to your liking, there's one fix that almost never fails: Pour some Champagne on it.

- **GO LARGE-FORMAT.** Think about hosting an aperitif party the same way you think about cooking a family-style meal: Batch your drinks ahead, and don't be afraid to let your guests serve themselves. A good rule of thumb is to batch two drinks per person for a cocktail hour and three for a cocktail party. (Consider anything left over your reward for being a smart host.) Leave a note on a pre-set cocktail table with a pitcher, a bowl of ice, and garnish for easy assembly.

◆ **DON'T FORGET THE SNACKS.** The aperitif cocktail wouldn't really exist without the ritual that goes alongside it, which is all about the act of grazing. Keep your aperitif spread simple: think cured meats or pâte, a selection of cheeses, topped crostini or tartines, and the like.

◆ **EMBRACE THE APERITIF LIFE.** Don't forget that the aperitif, or *l'apéro*, is more than a ritual—it's a state of mind. Embrace it.

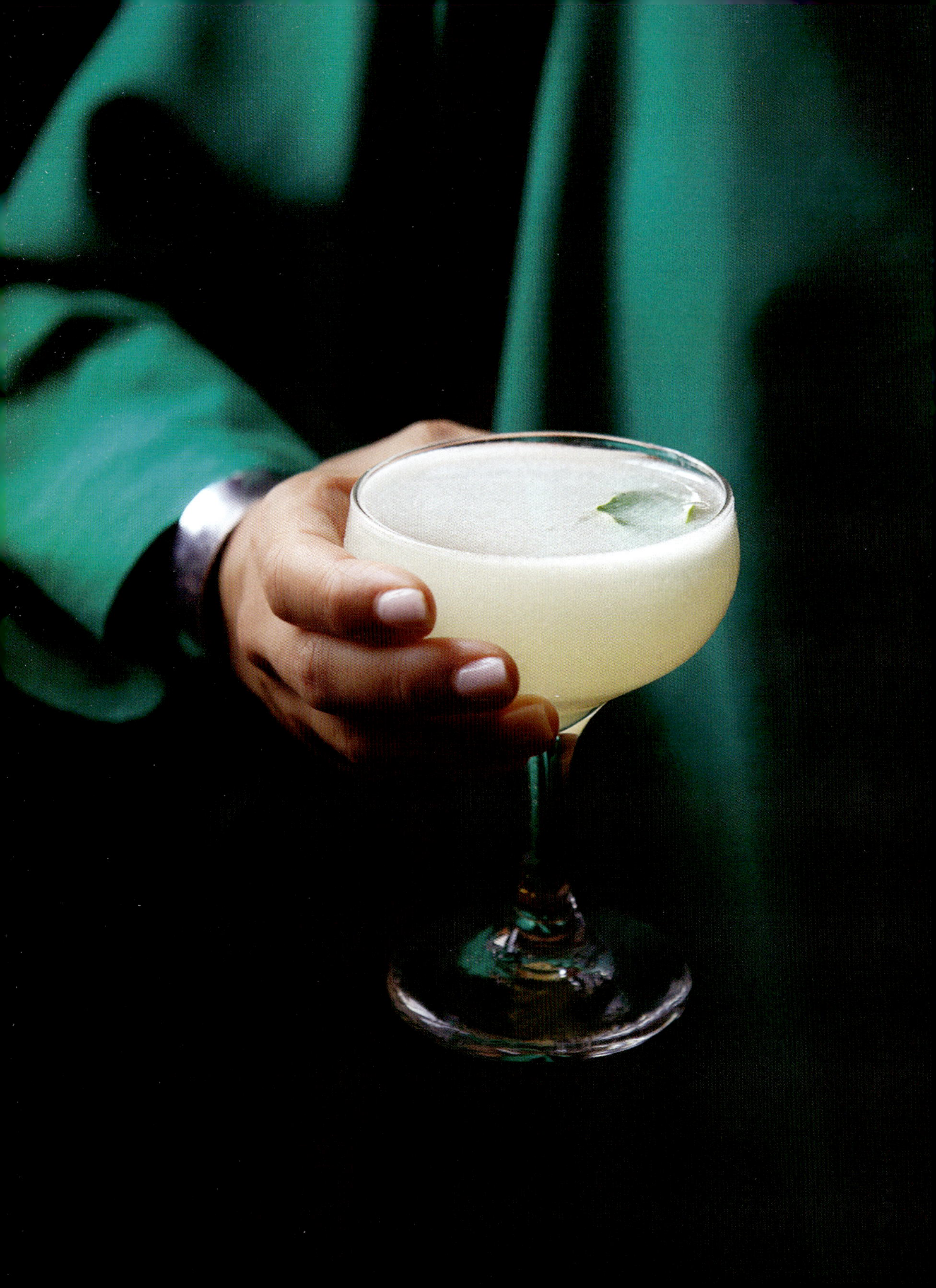

SERVES 1

Xavier Herit
—
Wallflower

TÊTE-À-TÊTE

CRAFTED WITH CITADELLE GIN and *St-Germain*, the central components of Xavier Herit's Tête-à-Tête nod to the bartender's own French roots, while the flavor profile sticks to the classic combination of elderflower and cucumber.

1½ ounces **premium French gin**
¾ ounce **St-Germain**
¾ ounce **lime juice**
¼ ounce **simple syrup (1:1, sugar:water)**
¼ ounce **cucumber juice (see page 152)**

GLASS

GARNISH Basil leaf and 3 cubeb peppers

METHOD Shake all of the ingredients with ice and strain into a coupe. Garnish with the basil leaf and cubeb peppers.

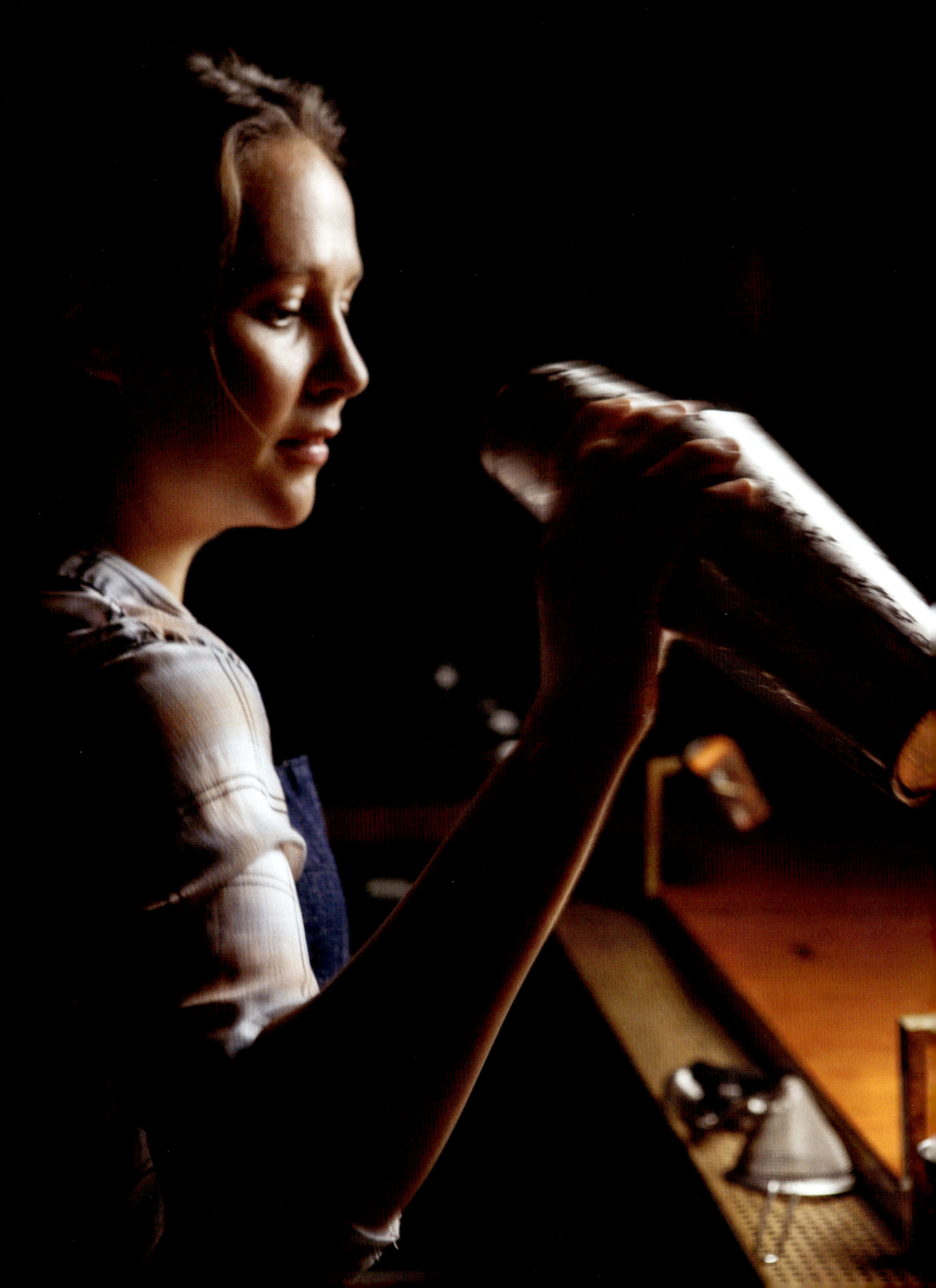

DINNER

CULINARY COCKTAILS 104

MISE EN PLACE 110

PAIRING COCKTAILS WITH FOOD 116

RECETTES

Voodoo Down 106 ◆ *Darlin' Don't Refrain* 109
Keystone Highball 113 ◆ *Smoked Tomato* 114 ◆ *The Hudson Glacier* 118
Fiore di Francia 121

COCKTAILS HAVE ALWAYS HAD A COMPLICATED RELATIONSHIP WITH FOOD.

WINE? SURE. But the conventional thinking with cocktails was that they were too strong to pair with a good meal, and should be enjoyed on their own. Lucky for us, this lazy logic has begun to crumble, encouraging drink-makers across the nation to think more critically about how cooking complements cuisine and vice versa.

In the earliest days of his career, Eleven Madison Park and The NoMad bar director Leo Robitschek felt the divide. Back then, "Chefs didn't like sharing, nor did they like sharing their tools," he says. "They also didn't like to be outshined." After joining the EMP team, however, Robitschek found an enthusiastic collaborator in Daniel Humm, a chef eager to build trust between the cooks in the back and the bartenders working out front. Members of Humm's staff would sit in on Robitschek's weekly tastings, both to share feedback and to gather ideas for use in the kitchen.

This kind of dialogue has become increasingly commonplace. "Through my career, I've seen the culinary arts advance and craft cocktails become prevalent in restaurants, and because of that there's a lot more collaboration," says Julian Cox, beverage director of the Chicago-based Lettuce Entertain You. "Now we're literally working hand in hand to create entire menus together and exchange ideas."

Such synergy has helped blur the line between chef and bartender, ultimately elevating both the restaurant and bar industries. What kick-started this new attitude toward collaboration? Some bartenders attribute the uptick to heightened consciousness across the industry at large—chefs are much more visible now thanks in part to the popularity of food TV, and their focus on ingredients is increasingly *en vogue*. "It was the continued growth of hospitality in general," says Abigail Gullo, bartender at Compère Lapin in New Orleans. "We've seen the craft beer movement grow; we've seen the farm-to-table movement grow. It's all connected to what we do on the bar side."

Will Elliott, of Brooklyn's Maison Premiere and Sauvage, agrees. "As that element of locavorism and producer-driven experiences become more popular, you're definitely seeing bars follow suit," he says. Elliott has also levied bonds in the wine world to solidify this relationship. "Gaining the respect of wine people opens [cocktail bartenders] up to gaining the respect of kitchens and chefs."

The strengthened link between kitchen and bar manifests itself in the form of intelligent beverage pairings, but it's also influenced how bartenders work, both physically and creatively. "When I first started bartending, it was always the kitchen versus front-of-house. Now it's much more of a conversation," says Ezra Star of Boston's Drink. "The kitchen has become more of a centerpiece and a place for inspiration."

Star and her staff tap the chefs of sister restaurants Menton and No. 9 Park for techniques and tools that will help them whip up proprietary cocktail additions, like syrups and cordials, more efficiently. But the core connection between chef and bartender runs deeper than technique. Star's Fiore di Francia is a potable nod to Franco-Italian relations, encouraging Gallic *St-Germain* and Italian Cynar to align. "The cocktail was inspired by the food combinations I've seen along the Italian and French border, where elderflowers grow," she says. "The food is neither French nor Italian, but something in between."

This process also helps bartenders follow the lead of chefs and sync their ingredients to the seasons. At New York City's Mace, for example, the cocktails are classified not by style, strength, or spirit, but by spice—kitchen staples like coriander seed, fennel seed, star anise, and saffron dictate the makeup of their list. When

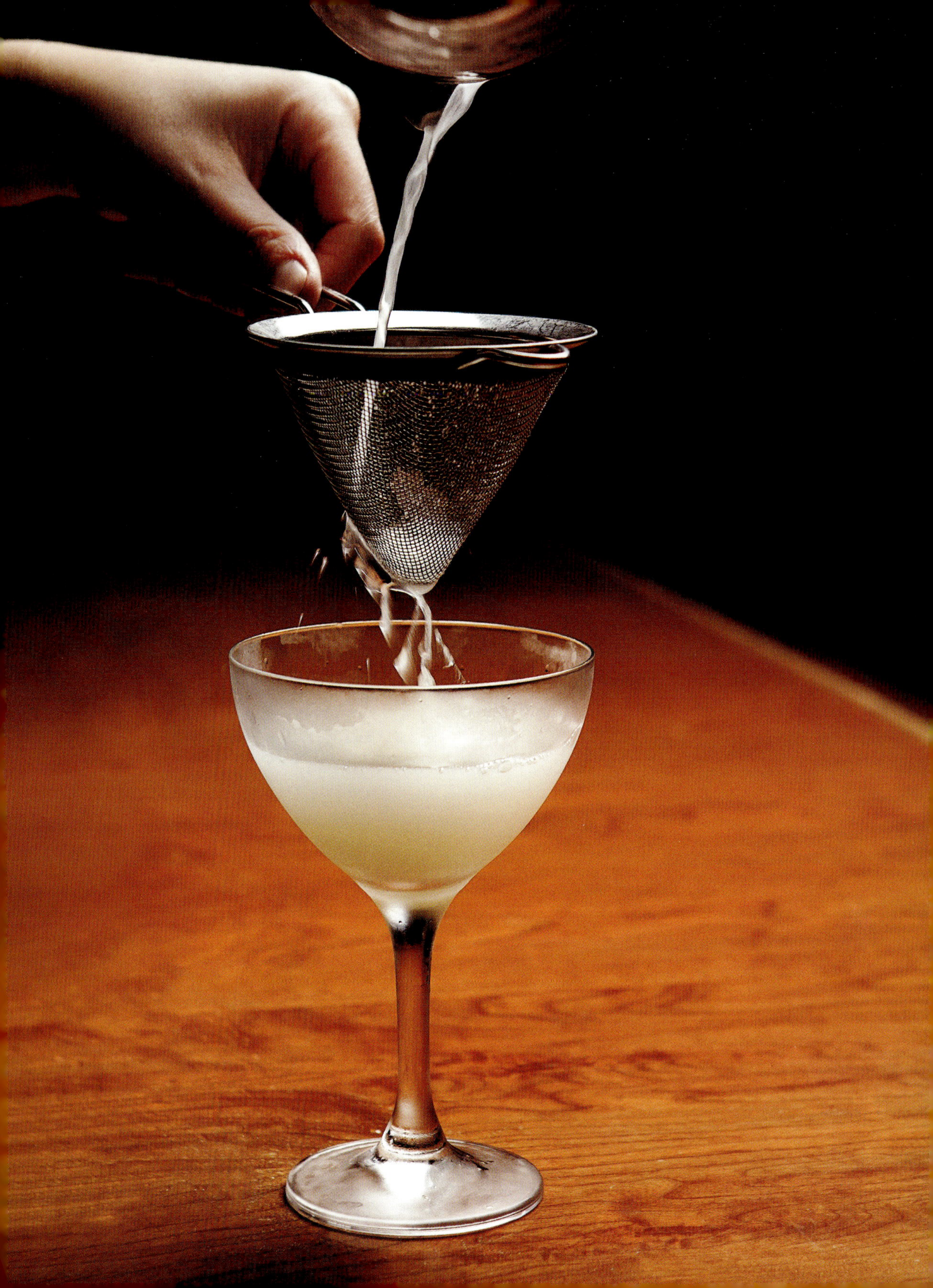

customers first came across the unorthodox menu, "They were surprised—but they were surprised in a good way," says co-owner Nico de Soto.

Bartender Matthew Biancaniello is so inspired by the culinary potential of cocktail-making that he's turned his experimentations into a career. His book, *Eat Your Drink*, teaches readers how to apply farm-to-table ethos to beverages; he also collaborates with chefs to create drinks, often based on savory, vegetal flavors, to match tasting menus. "My passion is more about the ingredients than the alcohol," he says. That passion is on fullest display in drinks like his Smoked Tomato, built around *St-Germain* infused with the curveball flavor of smoked height-of-season tomatoes. "*St-Germain* has a great flowery and sweet flavor, [which is] so much fun to play with," says Biancaniello. "The result is the *St-Germain* in the background with a unique smoky barbecue flavor in the front. So unexpected and so instantly inviting."

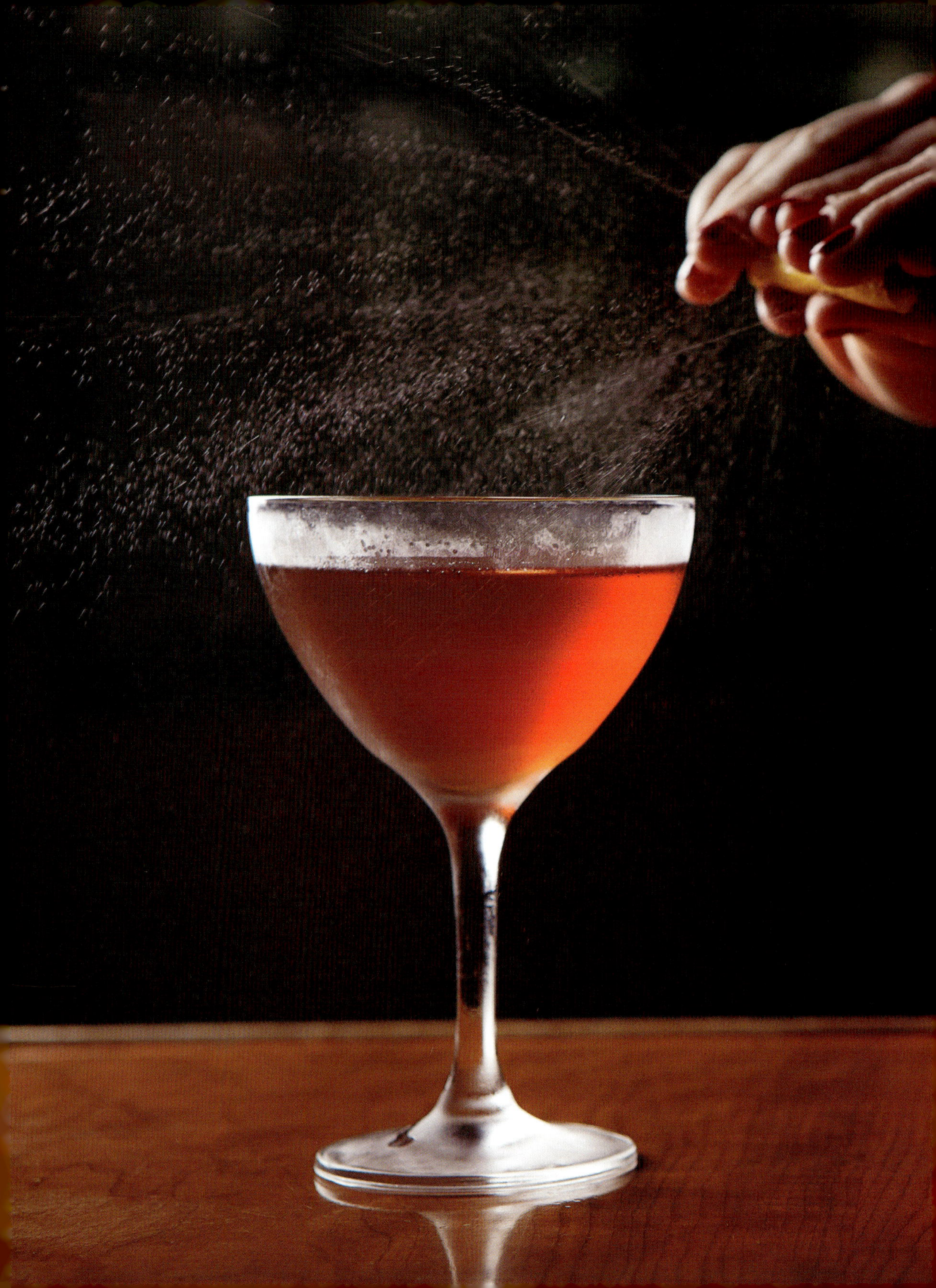

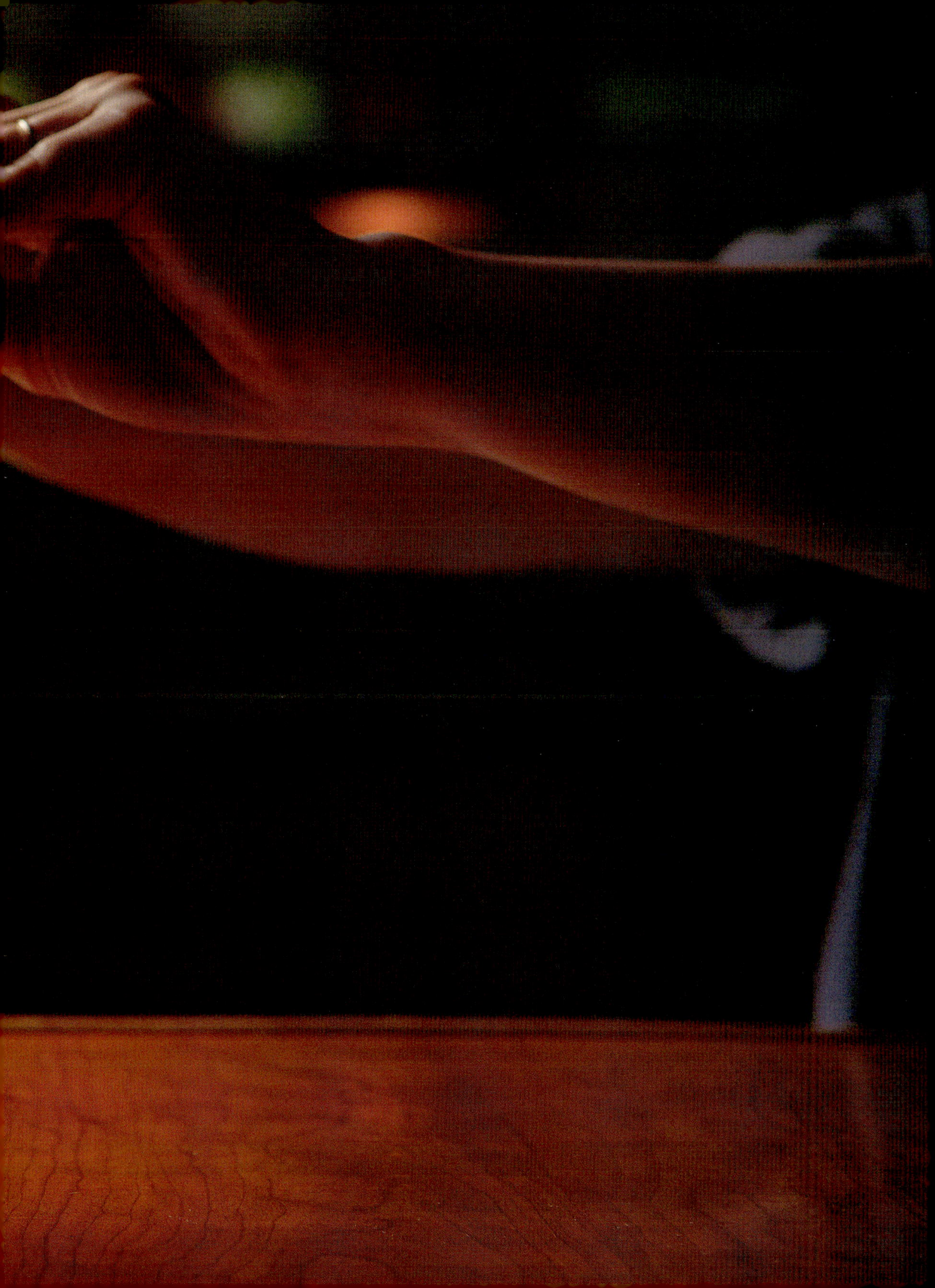

CULINARY
COCKTAILS

Cocktail bartenders take cues from their kitchen coworkers in a number of ways. The first and most obvious is that many tasks employed by bartenders during prep are identical to what their kitchen compatriots are getting into. "Housemade tinctures, syrups, bitters . . . all those are essentially cooking processes," says Micah Melton, beverage director of The Aviary, who worked as a cook prior to migrating over to the bar side. Sous vide, to name just one cooking technique with relevance on both sides, can be employed as a time-saving mechanism to speed up cocktail infusions.

"There's an incredible amount of crossover," says Julia Momose, head bartender of GreenRiver in Chicago. The idea of the "culinary cocktail" has long been rooted in the West Coast style of bartending, championed by pioneering San Francisco bartenders like Duggan McDonnell, Marco Dionysos, and Scott Beattie. It was, essentially, the farm-to-table approach to drink-making, which emphasized fresh produce and housemade syrups. Today this approach is a basic tenet of the craft cocktail movement worldwide. Phase two for the "culinary cocktail" has been more about an embrace of modernist techniques alongside a dedication to fresh ingredients.

At GreenRiver, for example, strong knife skills are a must for Momose's staff, as they are essential for creating beautiful, consistent, and functional garnishes—something Momose is known for. "A garnish should be an integral part of the drinking experience," she says. Some of her past tricks include cachaça-infused sugarcane dipped in white chocolate, and *pâte de fruit* dusted with the flavors of a Corpse Reviver.

For Matthew Biancaniello, who understands the intimate relationship between cooking and cocktailing better than most, the idea of the culinary cocktail is still rooted in where the bartender takes his or her inspiration. The author of *Eat Your Drink* is known for growing, foraging and scouring farmers' markets like a chef would to come up with ideas. "I still consider myself more in the food world than in the alcohol world," says the Los Angeles-based bartender, who has used everything from sea urchin and heirloom tomatoes to arugula and durian behind the bar. "It's all about ingredients first."

SERVES 1

Leo Robitschek
—
Eleven Madison Park

VOODOO
DOWN

NAMED AFTER THE Miles Davis song of the same name, Voodoo Down was born from an attempt to create a food-friendly Whiskey Sour. "The ginger and honey are really soothing for the stomach," explains Leo Robitschek. Likewise, the lemon and elderflower cleanse the palate, making it the ideal companion for dinner.

2 dashes **orange bitters**
¼ ounce **ginger syrup (1:1, ginger juice:turbinado sugar)**
¼ ounce **honey syrup (2:1, clover honey:water)**
¾ ounce **lemon juice**
½ ounce **St-Germain**
½ ounce **Trinidadian rum**
1 ounce **bourbon, preferably Elijah Craig 12-year**

GLASS

GARNISH None

METHOD Shake all the ingredients with ice. Strain over ice into a double rocks glass.

HOW TO DRINK FRENCH FLUENTLY ◆ 106

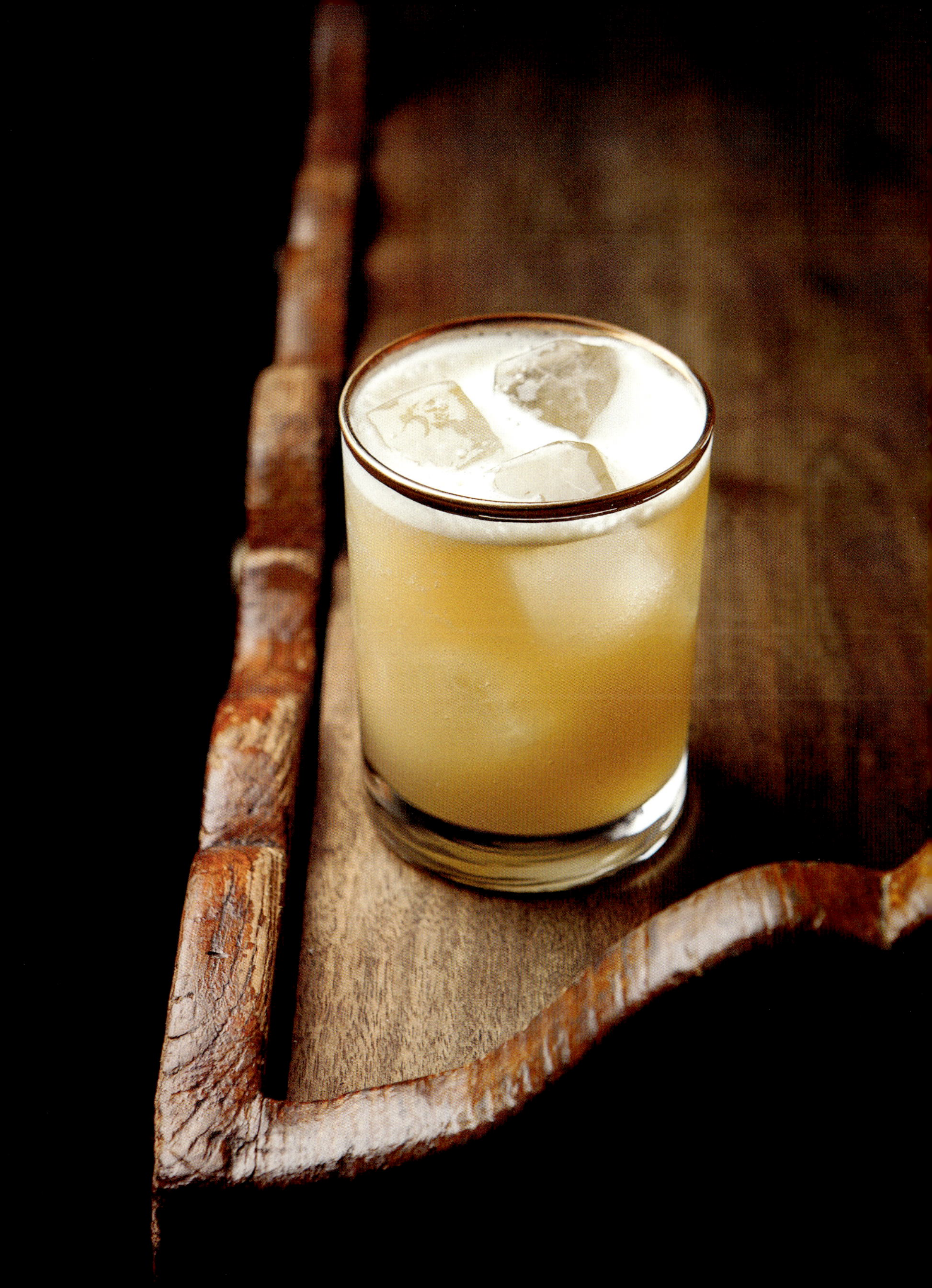

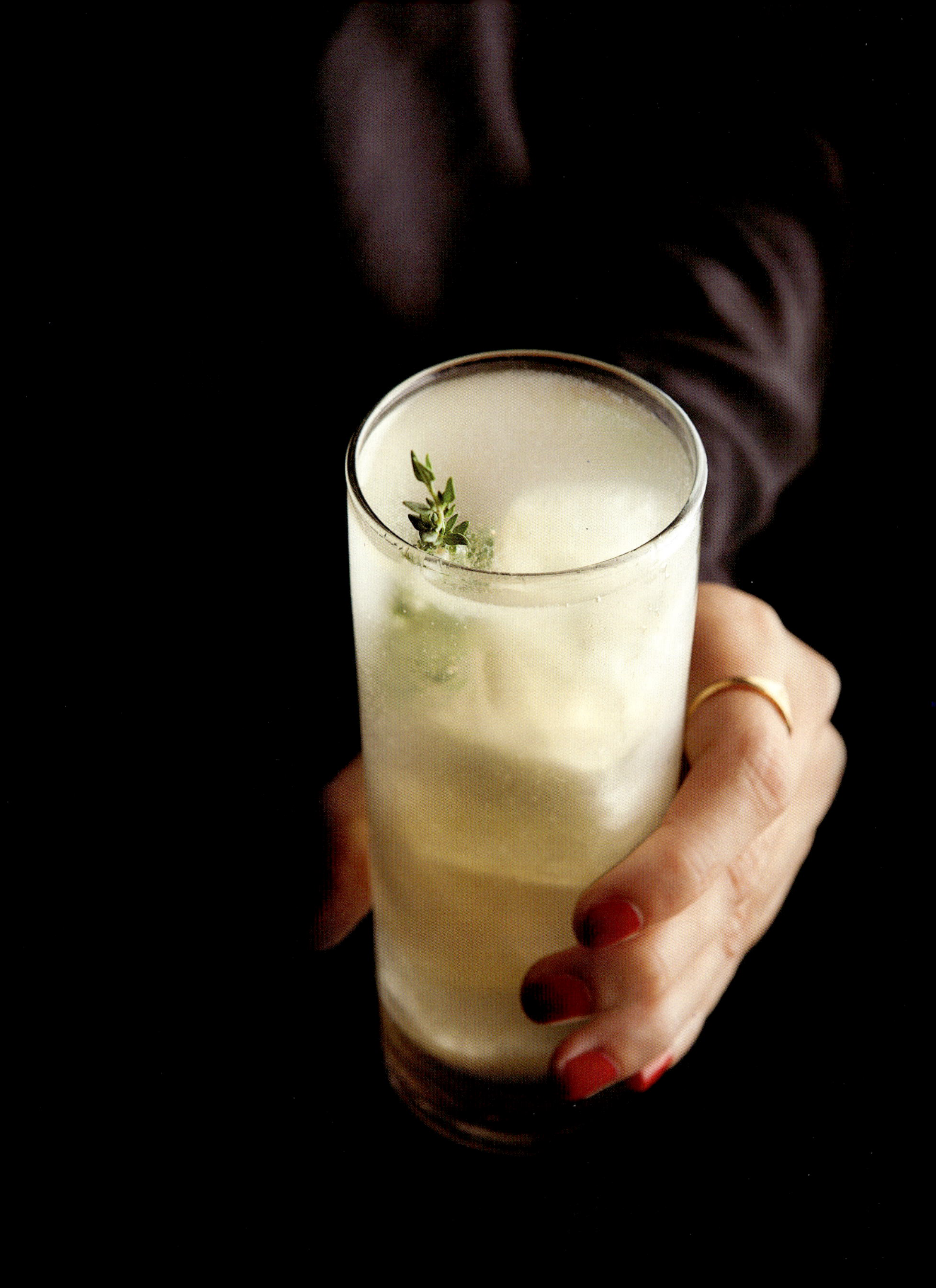

SERVES 1

Micah Melton — The Aviary

DARLIN' DON'T
REFRAIN

MICAH MELTON OFFERS A refreshing and vibrant drink with plenty of floral and citrus notes. Inspired by a recent trip to France, which included at least one spontaneous rendition of the classic power ballad "November Rain," Darlin' Don't Refrain reminds us to do just that: indulge. Keeping pace with the meal as it unfolds over the course of an evening, Melton's cocktail likewise develops over time as the elderflower ice cubes melt, adding new dimensions to the drink.

1½ ounces **London dry gin**
½ ounce **manzanilla sherry**
½ ounce **lemon juice**
¼ ounce **simple syrup (1:1, sugar:water)**
½ ounce **orange Curaçao, preferably BroVo**
3 drops **orange flower water**
3 *St-Germain* **elderflower ice cubes (see page 153)**
Soda water, to top

GLASS

GARNISH Fresh lemon thyme

METHOD In a shaker, combine all the ingredients except the *St-Germain* ice cubes and the soda water. Shake gently, then pour into a Collins glass filled with the *St-Germain* ice cubes. Top with the soda water and garnish with lemon thyme.

MISE EN PLACE

M*ise en place* is the rule of law on a restaurant line: everything has its place. The French term refers to a kitchen's meticulously organized tools and ingredients; it's how cooks keep order, cleanliness, and efficiency at peak levels during service. No surprise: The system so highly valued by chefs has practical applications behind the bar, as well.

"The design of our space itself allows us to operate as a kitchen, essentially," says Ezra Star, of Drink in Boston. A cocktail bar with no printed menus, Drink must be stocked with a formidable lineup of housemade drink modifiers—syrups, bitters, cordials, infusions, and the like—on top of its spirits selection, to accommodate customer requests.

Since space behind her bar comes at a premium, Star has to get creative with *mise*. Bottles, tools, and garnishes are stored below bar level to ensure that space remains uncluttered for customers; everything is organized in a systematic manner for the benefit of individual drink-makers. "We actually have stations designed like our kitchen stations, to produce cocktails the same way chefs would," she says. "Everything is extremely well-ordered, so it's standardized for our guests. Everything you need is within reach."

At Compère Lapin in New Orleans, bartenders sometimes show up a full five hours before their shifts begin to prepare their *mise*, which often overflows with seasonal fruits and herbs, the bounty of a year-round growing season. "The owners allowed us bartenders so much input," says bartender Abigail Gullo. "When it comes to how bars are normally set up, ours is extraordinary." For easy access, garnishes are stored in a box out of the customer's eyeline, "like the cockpit of a jet plane." Features like a rinser for cocktail tins, a glass chiller that doubles as a holding place for frozen garnishes, a centralized cluster of "low boy" fridges for ingredient storage, and a spacious prep area with its own refrigeration ensures that "all that we need is just a step away," says Gullo.

Meanwhile, at Chicago's The Aviary, which has a reputation for whimsical and highly elaborate drinks, staffers can show up as early at six a.m. to begin work for a five p.m. opening. "[*Mise en place*] is paramount here," says beverage director Micah Melton. Their goal of four-minute ticket times—the seconds elapsed between when an order is received and when it's delivered—requires "*a lot* of pre-preparation to make the experience appear seamless for our guests."

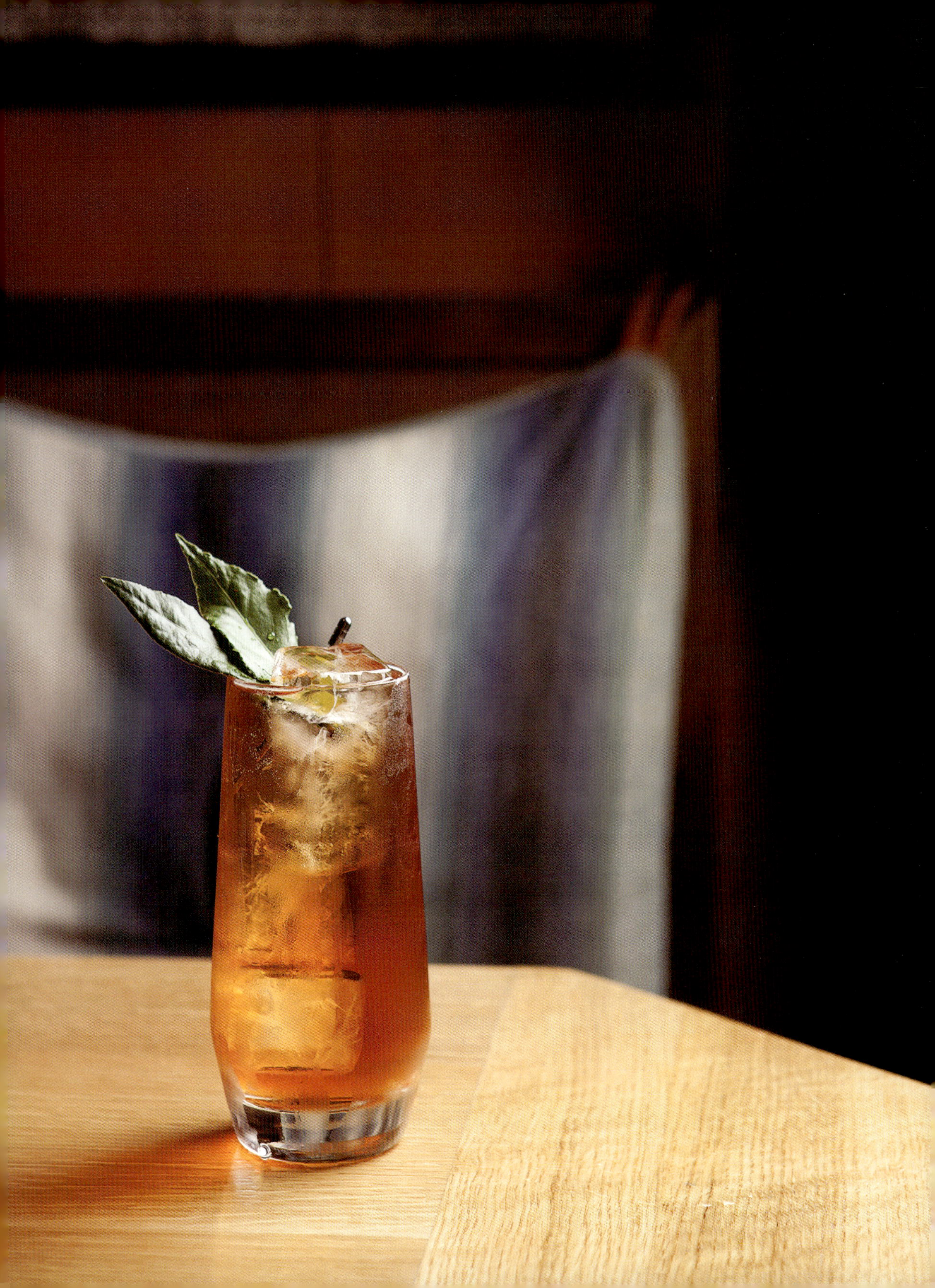

SERVES 1

Julia Momose
—
GreenRiver

KEYSTONE
HIGHBALL

"THIS COCKTAIL IS LIKE the keystone in a bridge," explains Julia Momose, who likens an evening of drinking to a bridge spanning from the aperitif to the nightcap, with the keystone falling right in the middle, with dinner. Like any thoughtful pairing, Momose's take on the dinner cocktail can be adjusted to suit the meal at hand: "When it comes to the garnish, this should never be an afterthought . . . rosemary, mint, thyme, oxalis, lavender . . . all of these may be beautiful accents to a special meal," she says.

½ ounce **mint tea (see page 153)**
½ ounce **St-Germain**
1½ ounces **whiskey, preferably Rieger's Kansas City**
4 ounces **soda water,** plus more to top

GLASS

GARNISH Lemon peel, fresh bay leaf (or another fresh herb to complement the meal)

METHOD Fill a highball or Collins glass two-thirds full with ice. Stir to chill the glass, then drain off any water. Pour the tea, *St-Germain*, and whiskey into the glass and stir gently to combine. Pour soda water down the side of the glass so as to retain carbonation. Add ice and top with a final splash of soda water. Express the lemon peel, then discard. Garnish with the fresh bay leaf.

SERVES
1

Matthew Biancaniello

SMOKED
TOMATO

"ST-GERMAIN HAS A GREAT flowery and sweet flavor that is so much fun to play with," explains Los Angeles–based bartender Matthew Biancaniello, who pairs the elderflower liqueur with elements pulled directly from the dinner table.

¾ ounce **lemon juice**
¼ ounce **agave syrup (see page 153)**
1½ ounces **pitted Santa Rosa plums**
4 **anise hyssop leaves**
2 ounces **smoked tomato–infused** *St-Germain* **(see page 153)**

GLASS

GARNISH Flowering garlic chives (or other edible flower)

METHOD In a shaker, muddle all of the ingredients except the infused *St-Germain*. Add the *St-Germain* and ice and shake. Double strain into a coupe and garnish with flowering garlic chives.

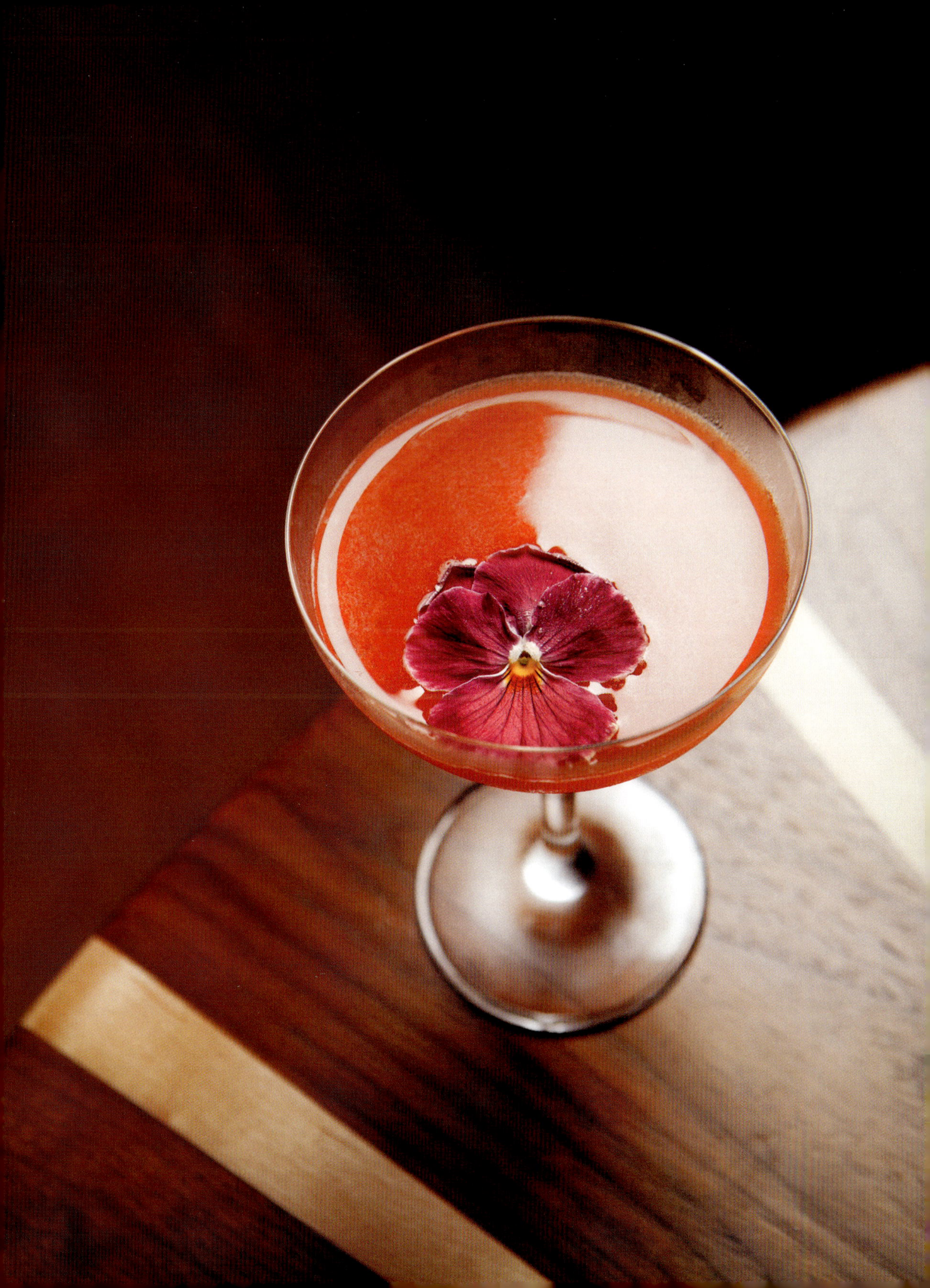

PAIRING
COCKTAILS WITH FOOD

Despite the significant advances craft cocktail culture has made in recent years, there are still many out there who firmly believe that pairing spirits with food is a fool's errand. Plenty of today's bartenders are here to tell you otherwise. "The idea that cocktails can't pair well with food is outdated," says Abigail Gullo of Compère Lapin. "Cocktails can absolutely be paired with food—you just have to very careful and precise." Here are five important rules to remember when working on a pairing.

- **OPPOSITES ATTRACT.** "If the cocktail is being prepared to accompany a dish, I always want to be sure to know how spicy or bold a dish is before pairing," says Julian Cox, beverage director of Lettuce Entertain You. "A lot of people try to match a cocktail menu to a food menu—I think it's better to complement."

- **SIMPLICITY IS SOPHISTICATION.** A multitude of flavors in a drink, served alongside a multitude of flavors on a plate, can often lead to confusion and palate exhaustion. "Drinkability is a huge element," says Will Elliott of Maison Premiere and Sauvage in Brooklyn. Though it seems to be counterintuitive to bartenders fond of complex drinks, a cocktail might "have to be a little plain Jane on the surface" to function efficiently in a pairing.

- **MIND THE SECONDARY FLAVORS ON A PLATE.** When his kitchen comes up with a new chicken dish, for example, Jay Bordeleau, of San Francisco's Maven, does not bother much with the meat itself. Instead he'll ask, "What's in the sauce? Flavor components of sauces and accouterments matter so much."

- **START OFF SUBTLE, THEN GET STRONGER.** When GreenRiver bartender Julia Momose designs a cocktail pairing for a multicourse meal, early cocktails will be "softer, lighter, and more nuanced," growing "richer and bolder" as the meal progresses toward conclusion.

- **BE PREPARED TO RIFF.** Tasked with a multi-drink pairing, Eleven Madison Park and NoMad Hotel bar director Leo Robitschek's drinks become highly customizable, and often so intertwined with the personality of the meal that the drinks wouldn't make sense solo. "There are cocktails we would do for a pairing that I would never serve as a singular cocktail in a bar setting," he says.

SERVES 1

Jay Bordeleau
—
Maven

THE HUDSON
GLACIER

FOR JAY BORDELEAU, THE key to a good dinner cocktail is keeping the alcohol content low while creating depth of flavor and intensity, all without compromising the balance of the drink. To tick these boxes, he floats a scoop of *St-Germain* sorbet on top of his dinner drink, where it slowly melts like a glacier in water, allowing the cocktail to evolve without dilution.

1 ounce **London dry gin**
1 ounce **Cocchi Americano**
¼ ounce **yellow Chartreuse**
½ ounce **lemon juice**
1 ounce **sparkling wine**
1 tablespoon ***St-Germain* sorbet** (see page 153)

GLASS

GARNISH None

METHOD Hard shake all of the ingredients with ice except the wine and sorbet. Double strain into a coupe. Float the sparkling wine on top and finish with the sorbet.

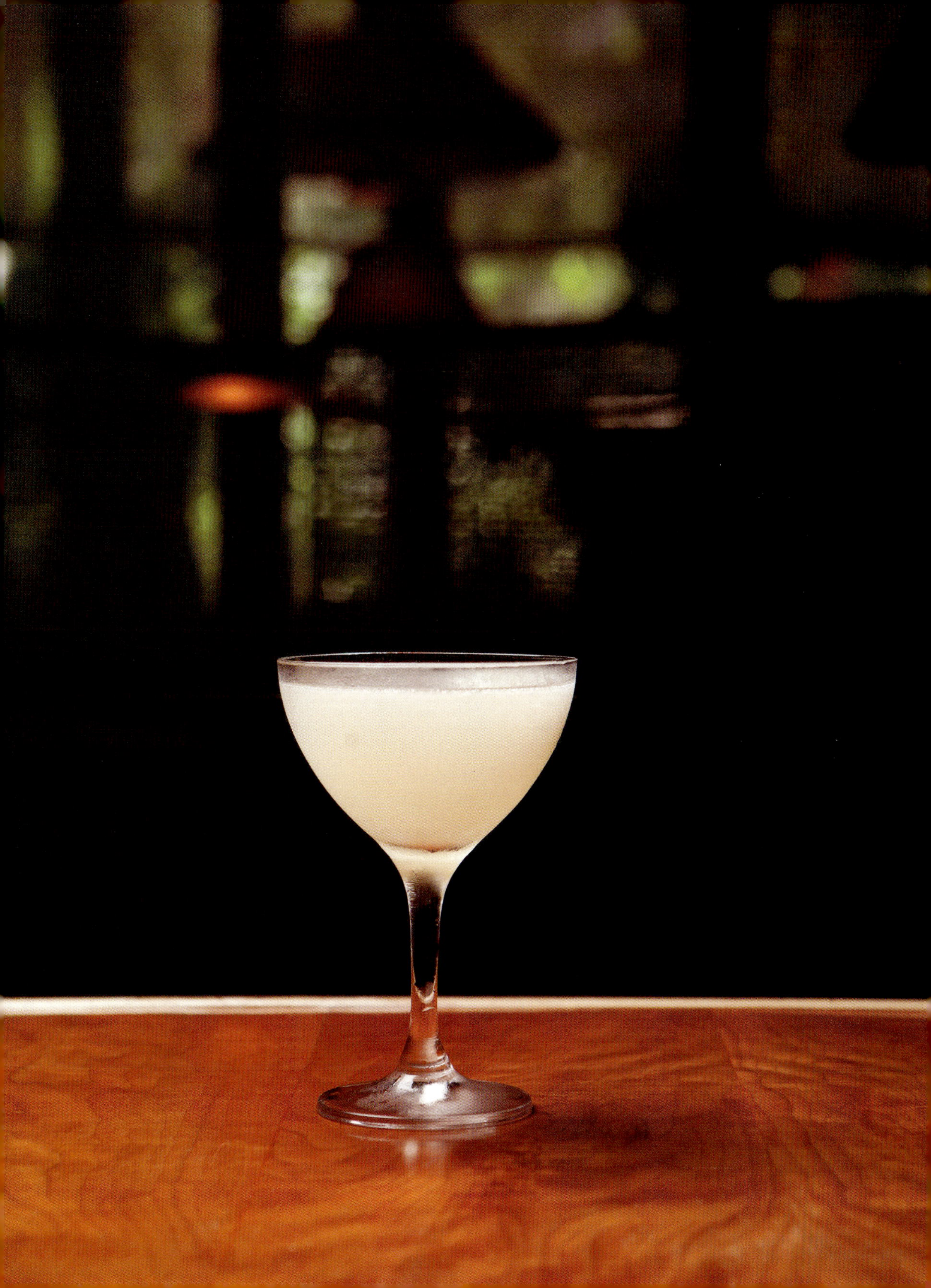

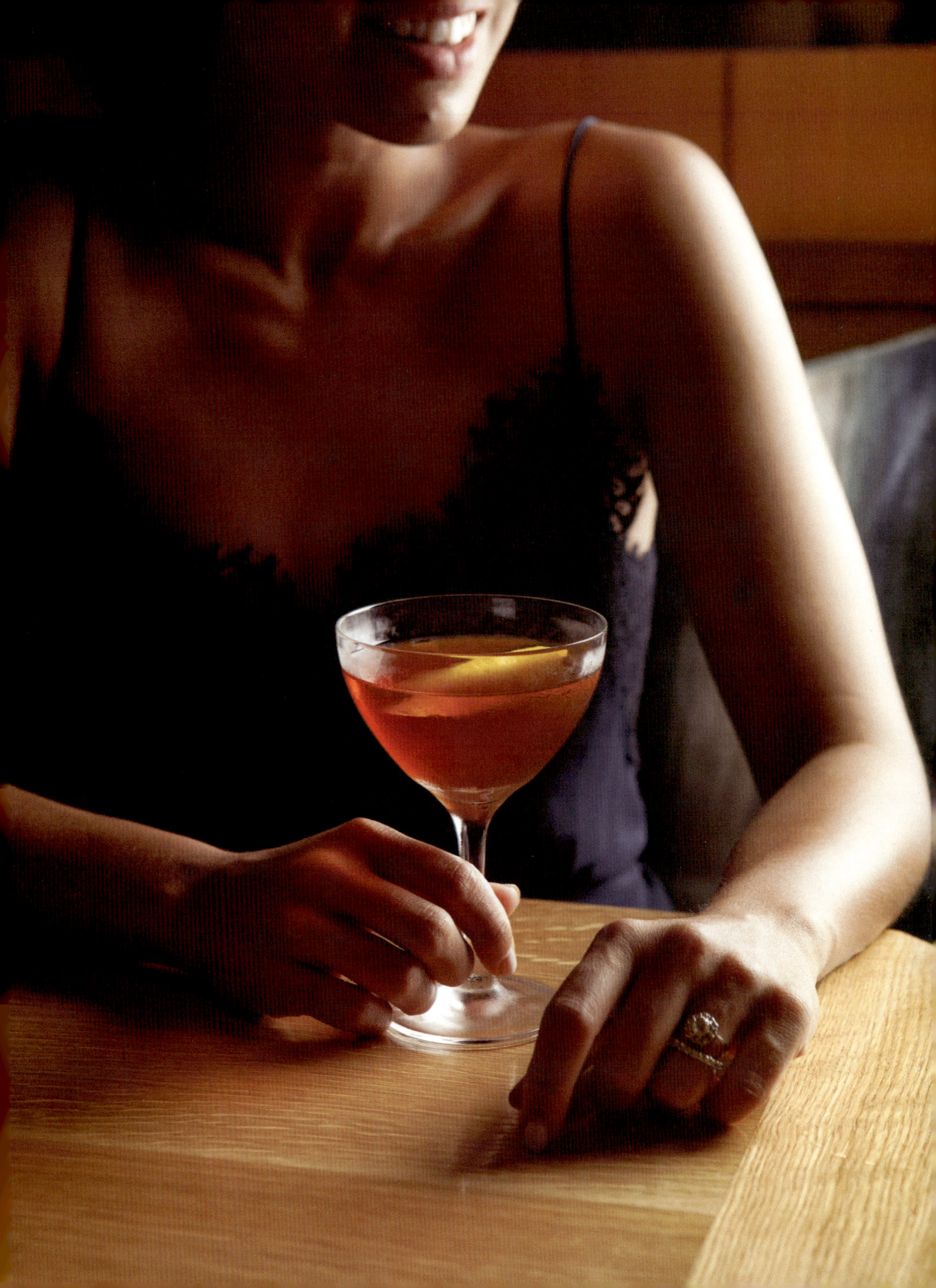

SERVES 1

Ezra Star — Drink

FIORE
DI FRANCIA

EZRA STAR FOUND INSPIRATION in the food encountered along the Italian and French border, where the cuisine belongs wholly to neither culture. Italian artichoke amaro, Cynar, joins forces with *St-Germain* in a nod to the border zone where elderflower grows freely.

1¼ ounces **blended whiskey**
1 ounce ***St-Germain***
¾ ounce **Cynar**
1 dash **Angostura bitters**

GLASS

GARNISH Lemon peel

METHOD Combine all of the ingredients in a mixing glass, add ice, and stir. Strain into a coupe. Express the lemon peel and discard.

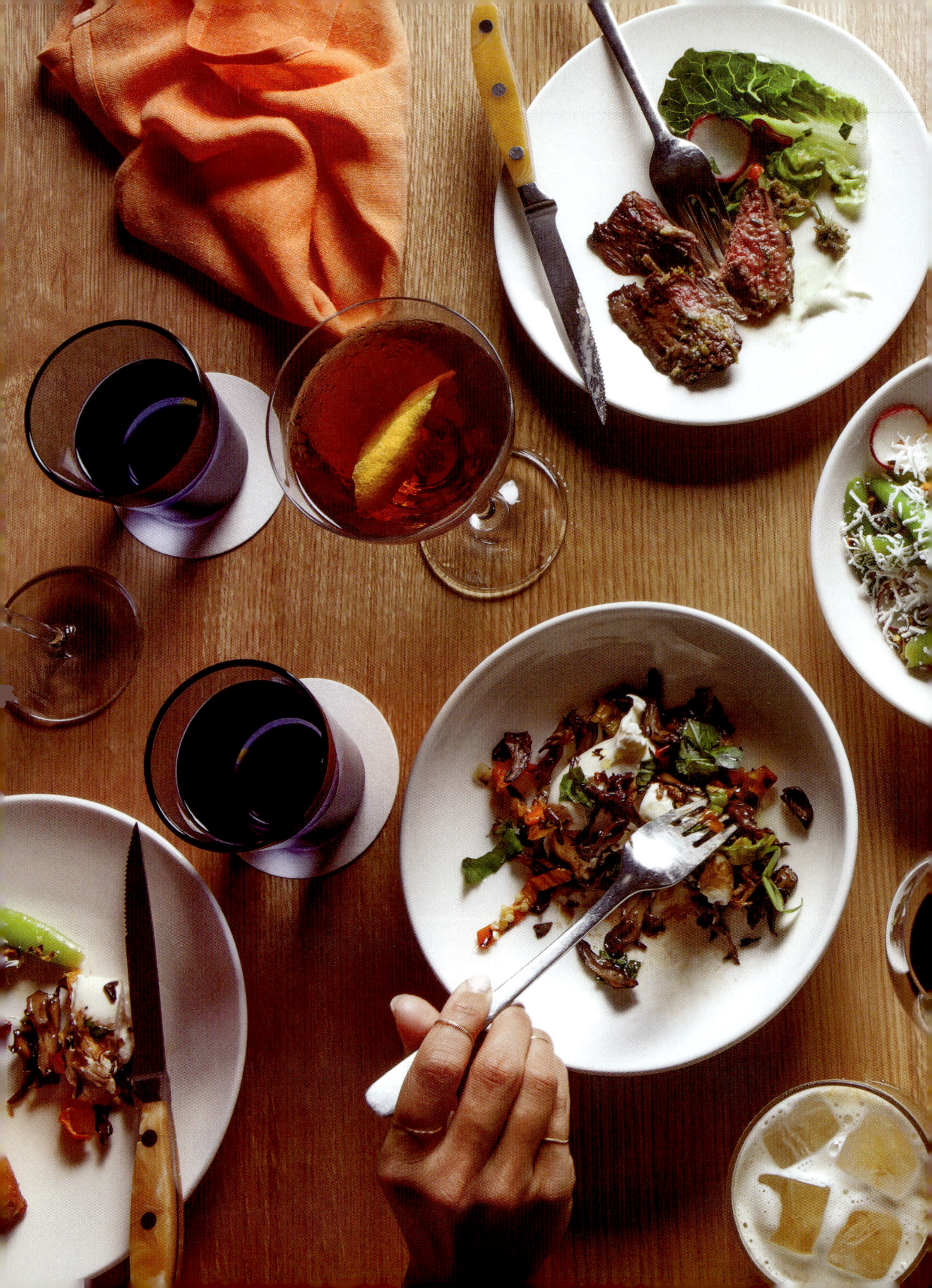

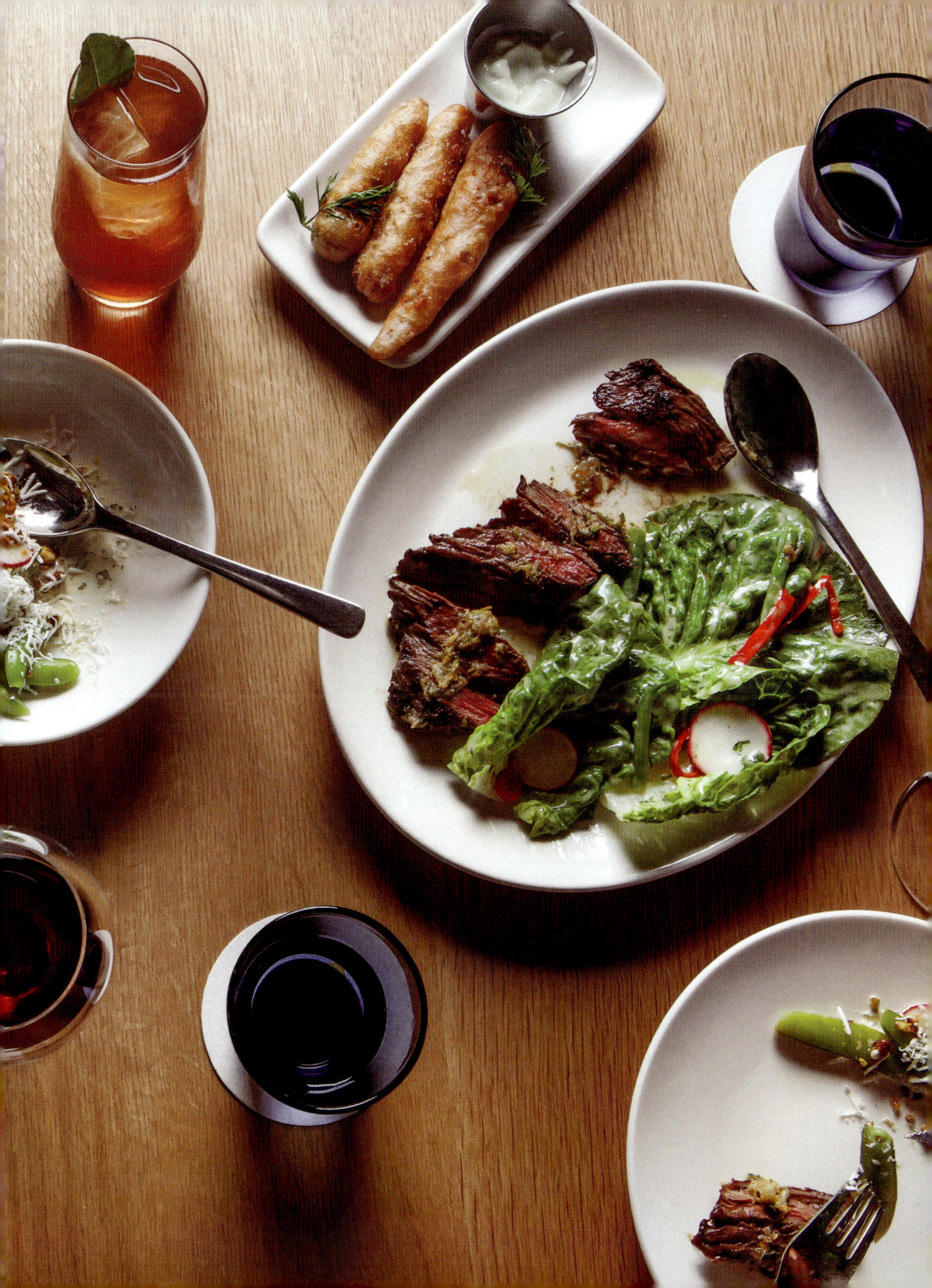

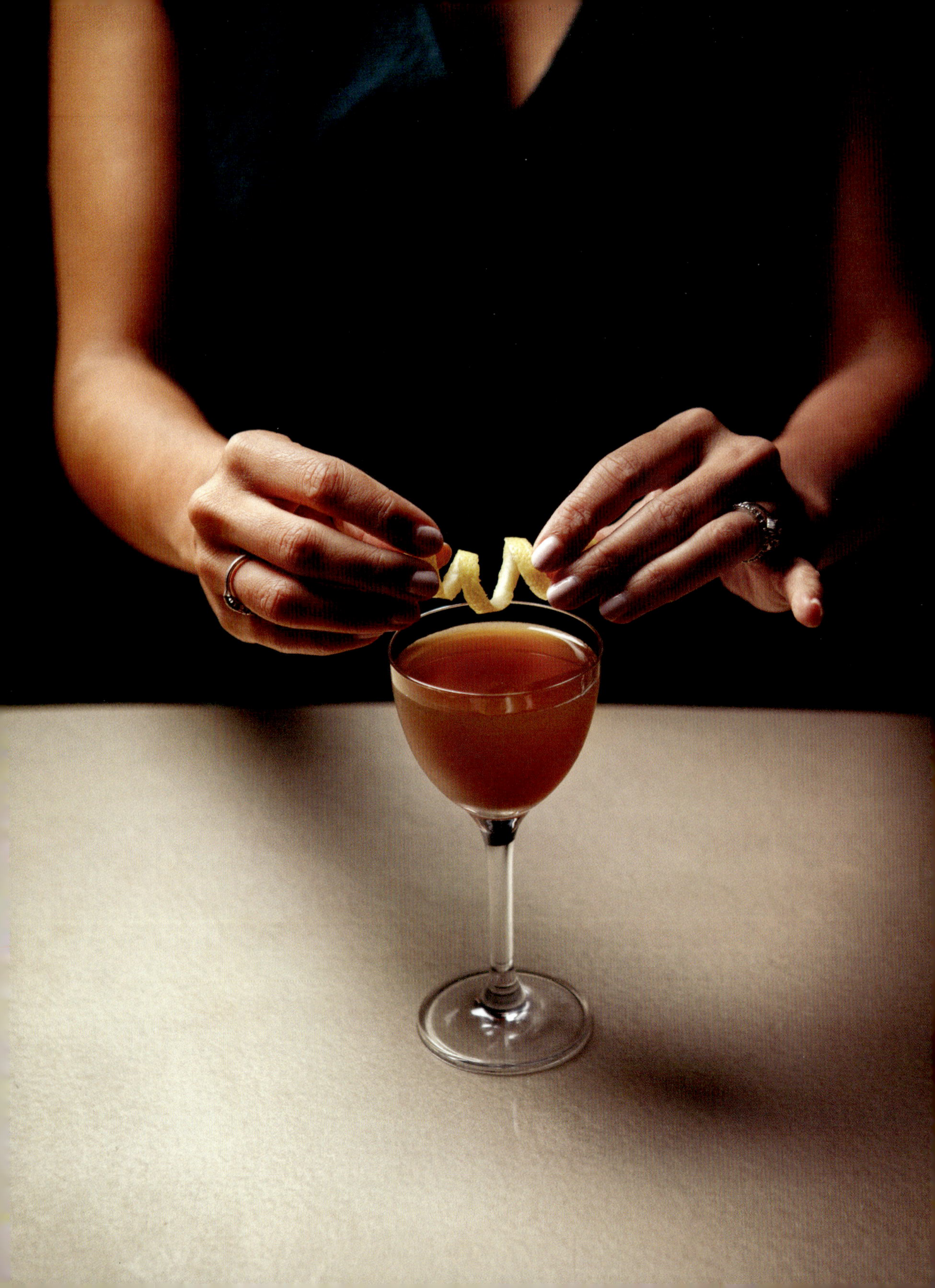

NIGHTCAP

ANATOMY OF A NIGHTCAP 136

BUILDING A NIGHTCAP BAR 142

RECETTES

Sailin' On 132 ◆ *Turn Down Service* 135
Midnight Bouquet 138 ◆ *Cooper's Nightcap* 141 ◆ *Lickety Split* 145
Duboudreau Cocktail 146

THE FINAL DRINK IS OFTEN THE ONE YOU FIXATE ON THE NEXT MORNING.

BASED ON TIMING ALONE, it has the power to make your evening one to remember—or one to regret. So why do so many of us take the nightcap for granted?

Though often used as a flimsy plot device in romantic comedies, the nightcap comes with both tradition and purpose. Aside from acting as a classy pin to stick in an evening, it's also an effective way to wind the night down—an elegant end to a night out, a gentle yielding instead of an abrupt stop. And bartenders, unsurprisingly, have a plethora of opinions on the matter—from what to drink to when and how to drink it. After all, as much as they facilitate nightcaps for others, their nights tend to conclude with one, too.

Conventional wisdom tells us a strong glass of something-or-other will send us quickly into a blissful dream state. But the nightcap has evolved; it's more than just a final drink. At its best, it's a category unto itself, with plenty of room for variation.

"*Nightcap* is a relative word," says Jim Meehan, owner of New York's PDT. "But it's certainly an important drink, because it's the last drink, it's the one that punctuates a night out." But what type of punctuation is most appropriate? A conventional period, wrapping things up all pert and professional? An ellipsis, casually lulling you off to Neverland? Or an exclamation point, ending the proceedings with a dramatic pop?

It's all of the above, of course. It just depends on who you ask.

"Nightcap, to me, puts me in a specific mind frame," says Karri Cormican, bartender at Wildhawk in San Francisco. "I want something a little bit stronger, heavy and distinct, to go out with a bang." Cormican manipulates this expectation in her Sailin' On (page 132), which augments a primary base of *St-Germain* with Galliano Ristretto and Fernet Branca. "The bright hints of herbs and mint balanced with the mellow coffee flavor make this cocktail a perfect end-of-the-night, slow-sipping cocktail," she says.

Dan Greenbaum, of New York's Attaboy, also tends toward darker, "more contemplative spirits," like high-end brandies or aged rums. He uses a whisper of *St-Germain*, along with 12-year-old Scotch and a touch of tawny port, to create the dessertlike Turn Down Service (page 135).

While a neat pour of a brown liquor or a simple boilermaker will often do the trick ("It doesn't have to be anything fancy," says Meehan), some bartenders around the country have gotten behind a growing trend: the low-alcohol, lighter-bodied nightcap. Moving toward options like sherries, vermouths, liqueurs, and cordials adds a manageable zip to the practice.

"For me, what makes a great nightcap is something that's going to leave me feeling satiated but also refreshed," says Kimberly Rosselle of San Francisco's Trick Dog, whose end-of-night go-tos include low-ABV favorites like spritzes and the Bamboo, a nineteenth-century classic involving equal parts vermouth and sherry, spiked with bitters. "There's been a strong shift among bartenders toward liqueurs," adds Rosselle, who's put a *St-Germain* boilermaker on Trick Dog's menu in response to the uptick.

Amari, too—whether on their own or mixed with an accompanying digestif—have their place among professional nightcap enthusiasts. "It's safe to say bartenders approach everything regarding alcohol differently than the consumer," says Seattle bartender Jamie Boudreau. "We're likely to go much more bitter." But since Boudreau's bar, Canon, is known nationwide for its extensive spirits selection, he doesn't have much trouble converting herbal-liqueur skeptics into his kind of drinker. "If they want one more, we usually direct them toward amaro," says Boudreau, who also replicates the sensation of amaro in his Cooper's Nightcap (page 141), a layered, Pousse Café–esque combo of chilled crème de mûre, Angostura bitters, and *St-Germain*.

With so many choices extending beyond strong, neat-poured spirits, the options for a proper nightcap in 2016 are nearly endless—and inclusive of both high- and lowbrow drinking tastes. Regardless of one's drink of choice, however, there's an unforeseen effect caused by today's plethora of nightcap options: the danger that "one more drink" can easily turn into two, three, or more. Which is why the first rule of the nightcap is that there is no *s* in nightcap.

"Ask for your bill with the last drink," advises Greenbaum. "That's a good way of policing yourself."

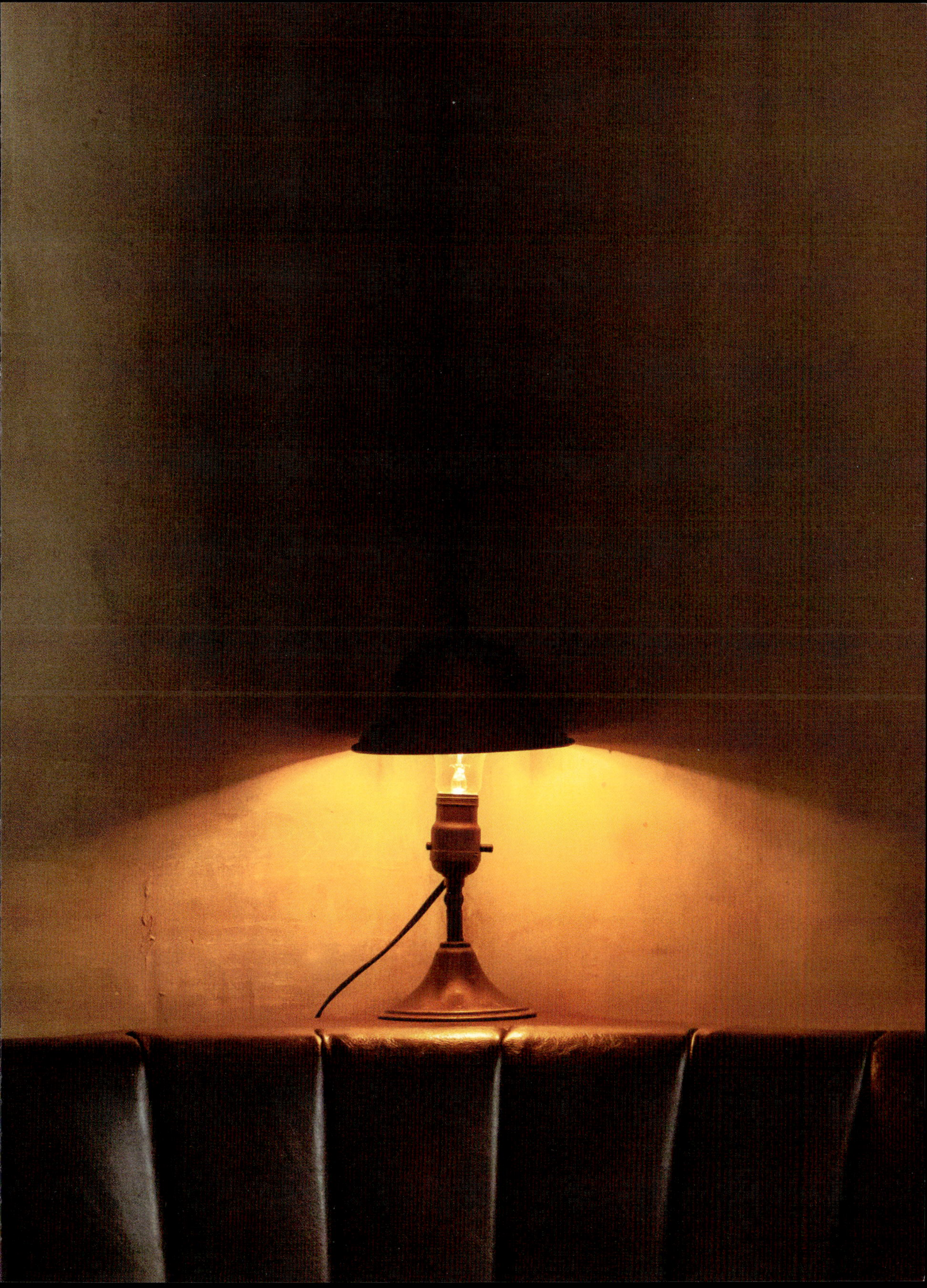

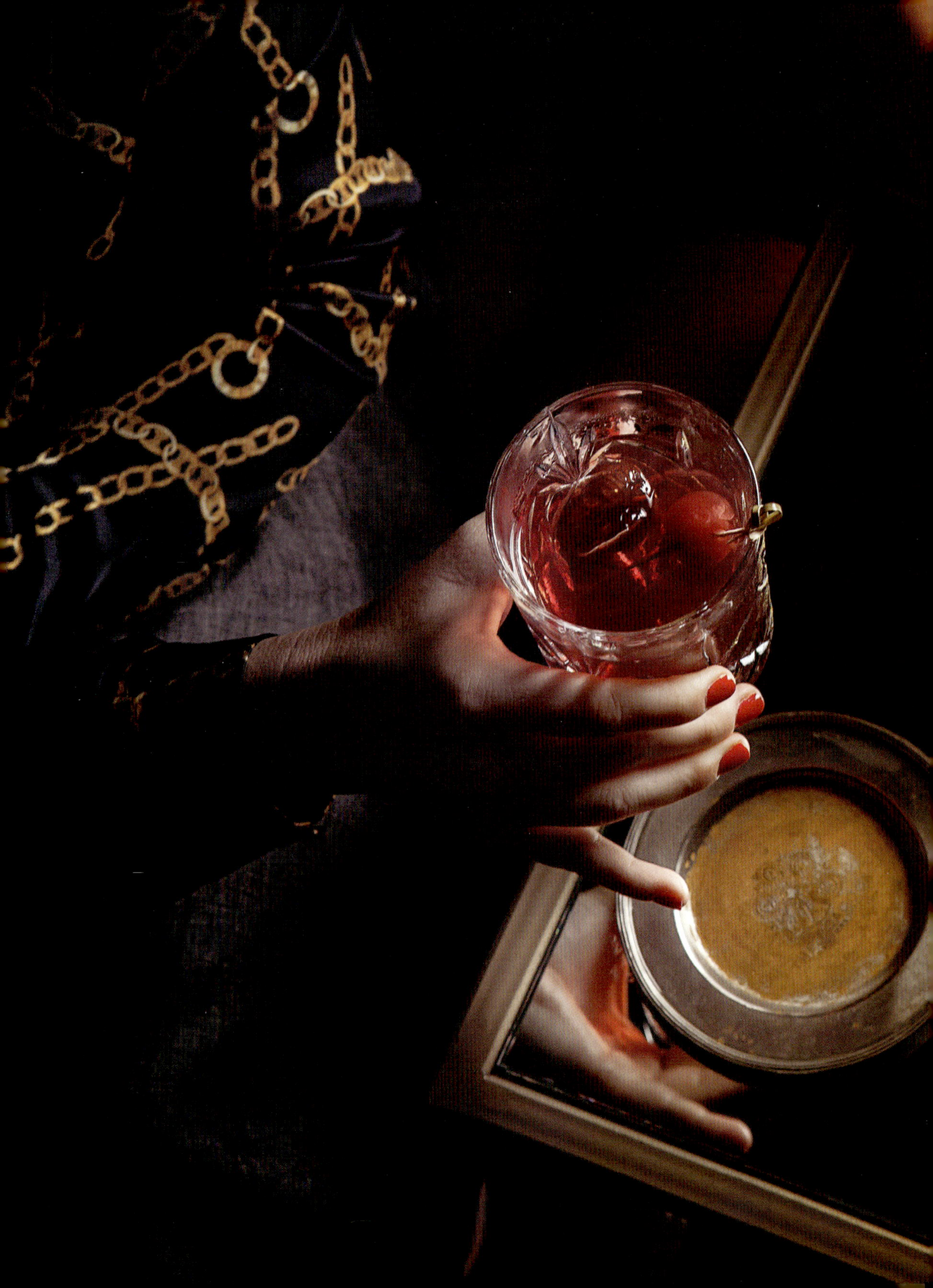

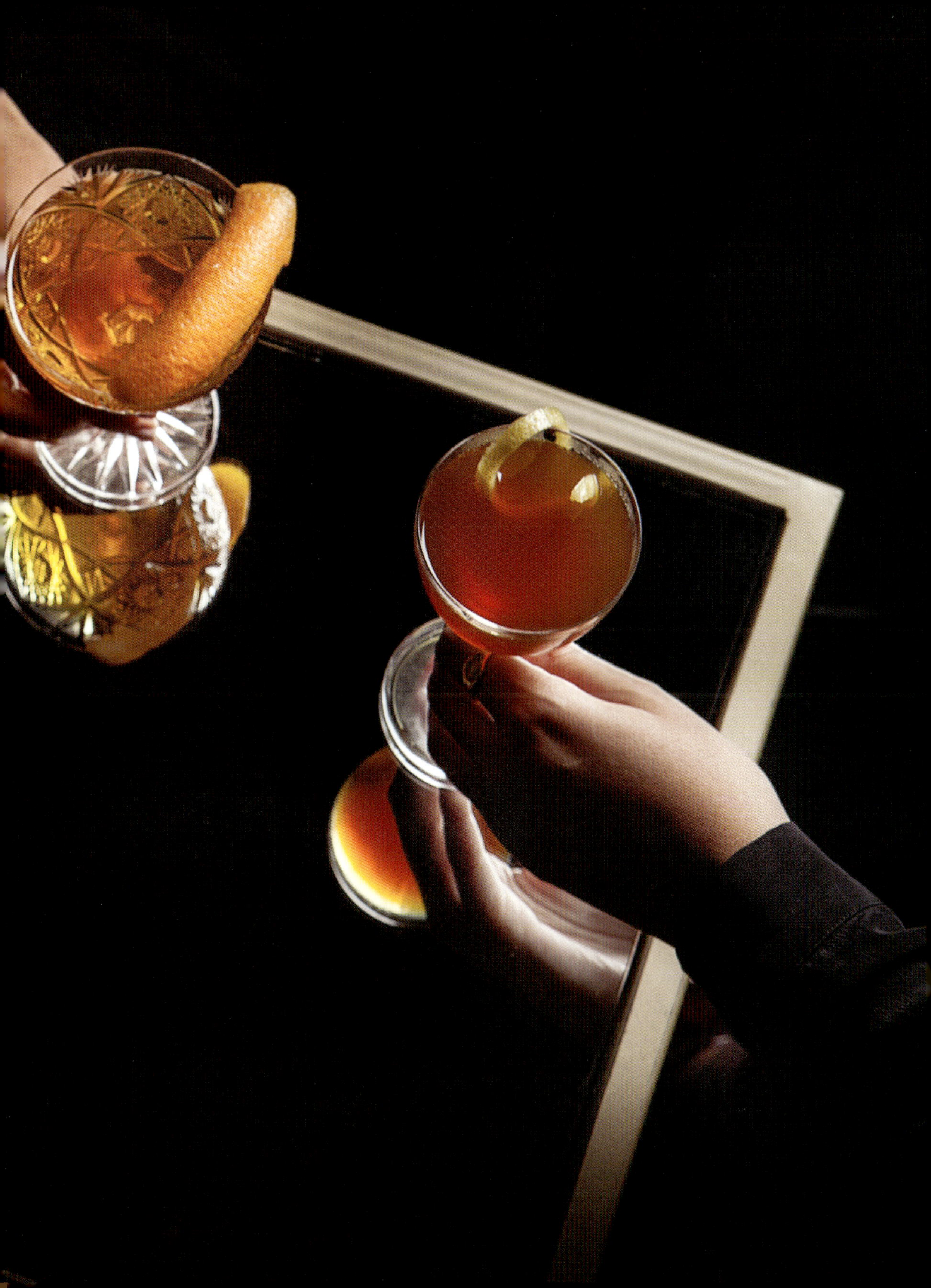

SERVES
1

Karri Cormican
—
Wildhawk

SAILIN' ON

KARRI CORMICAN'S TAKE ON a nightcap fuses the traditions of the after-dinner coffee and the digestif. The mellow coffee flavor of Galliano Ristretto balances the bright notes of herbs and mint of *St-Germain* and Fernet Branca to form a sipping cocktail that will keep the night sailing on.

2 ounces **St-Germain**
¾ ounce **Galliano Ristretto**
¼ ounce **Fernet Branca**

GLASS

GARNISH Orange twist

METHOD Stir all of the ingredients in a mixing glass with ice. Strain into a coupe. Garnish with the orange twist.

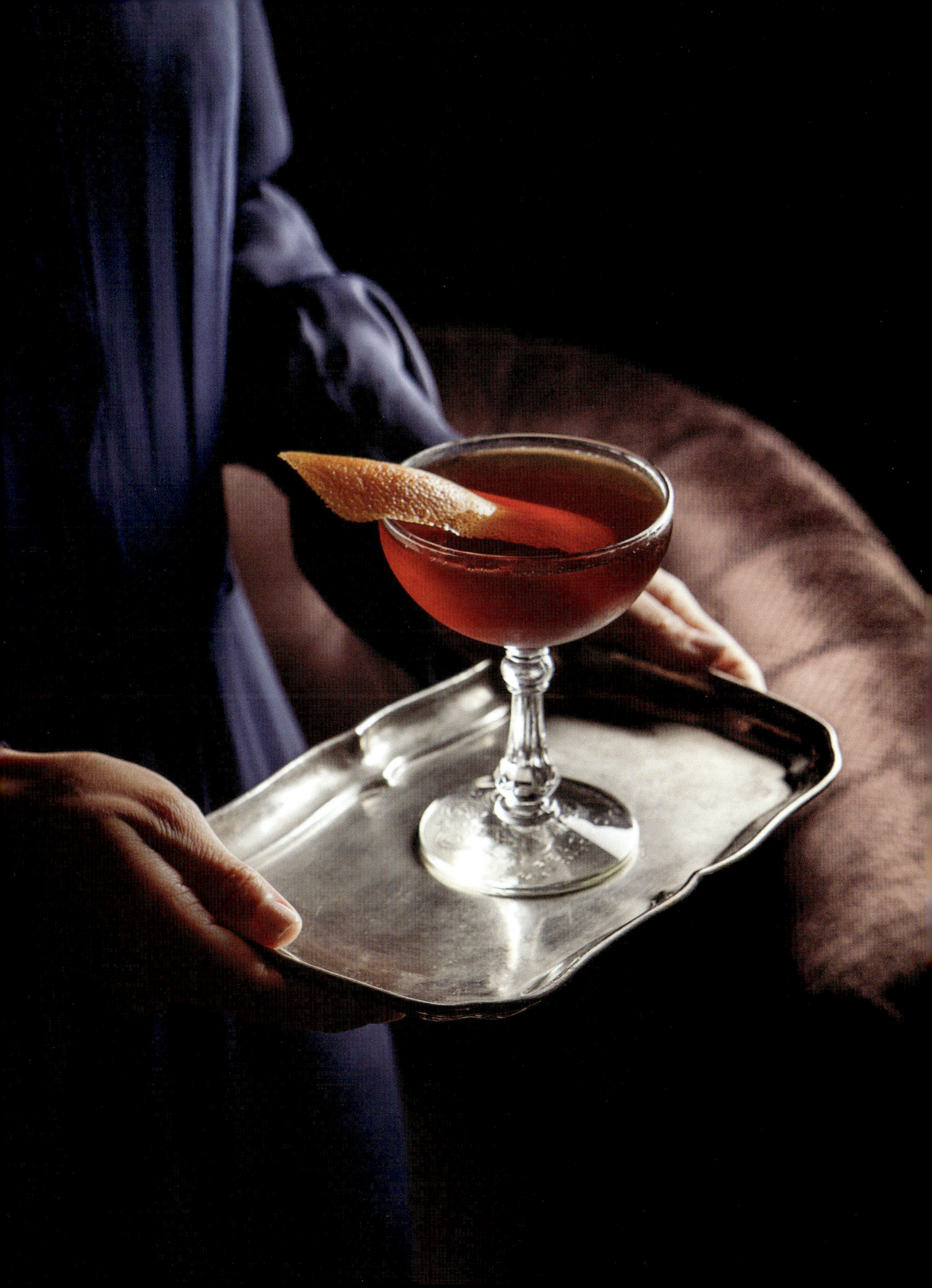

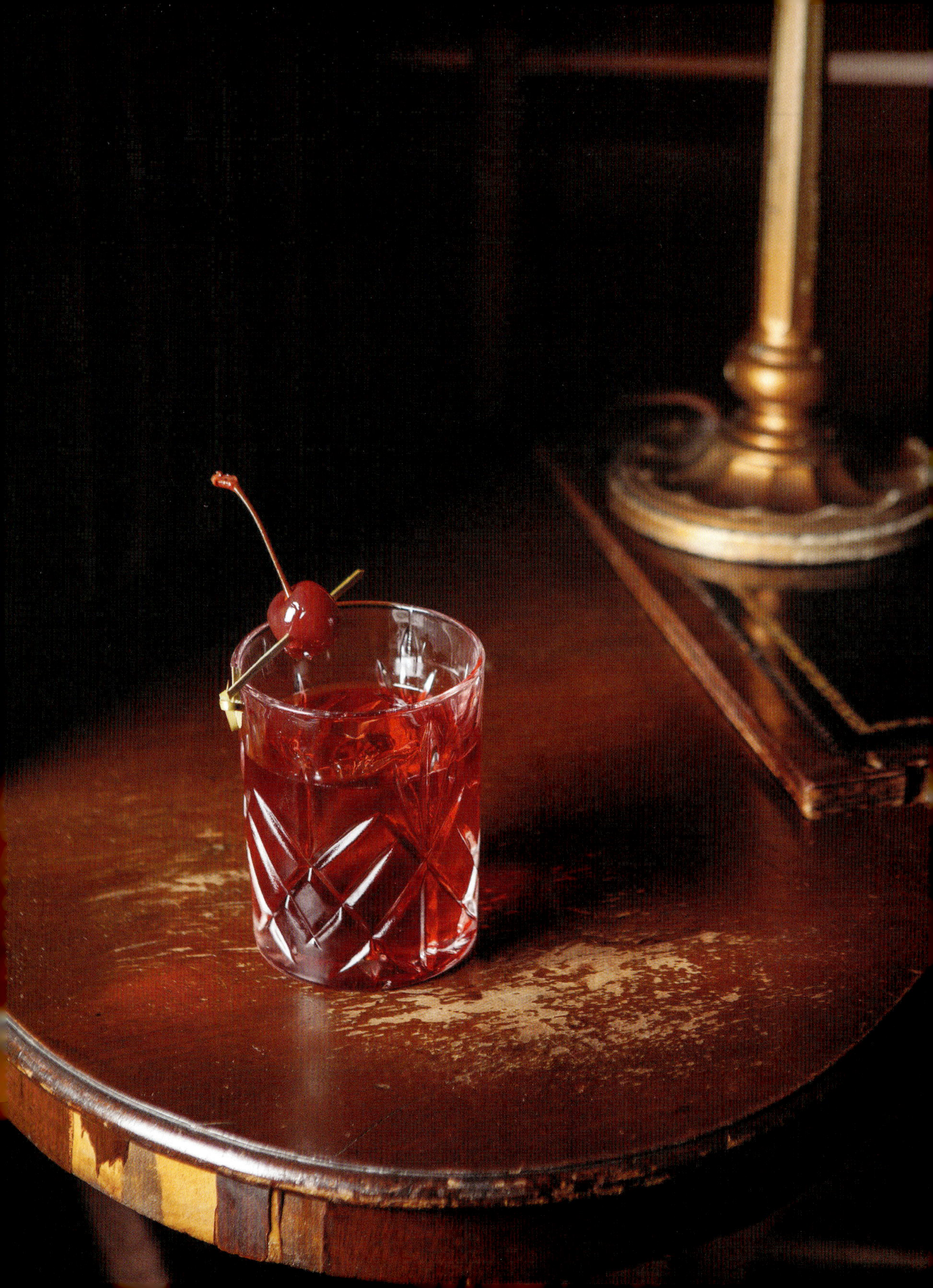

SERVES 1

Dan Greenbaum
—
Attaboy

TURN DOWN
SERVICE

DAN GREENBAUM'S TURN DOWN Service is, as the name implies, that final treat before turning in, like the chocolate on your hotel pillow. With just a touch of *St-Germain* alongside Scotch and tawny port, this spirit-forward drink is the final indulgence of the day, complete with the requisite cherry on top.

2 ounces **peated Scotch**
Scant ½ ounce ***St-Germain***
½ ounce **tawny port**

GLASS

GARNISH Cherry

METHOD Add all of the ingredients to a mixing glass, add ice, and stir. Strain over a large ice cube into a double rocks glass, and garnish with the cherry.

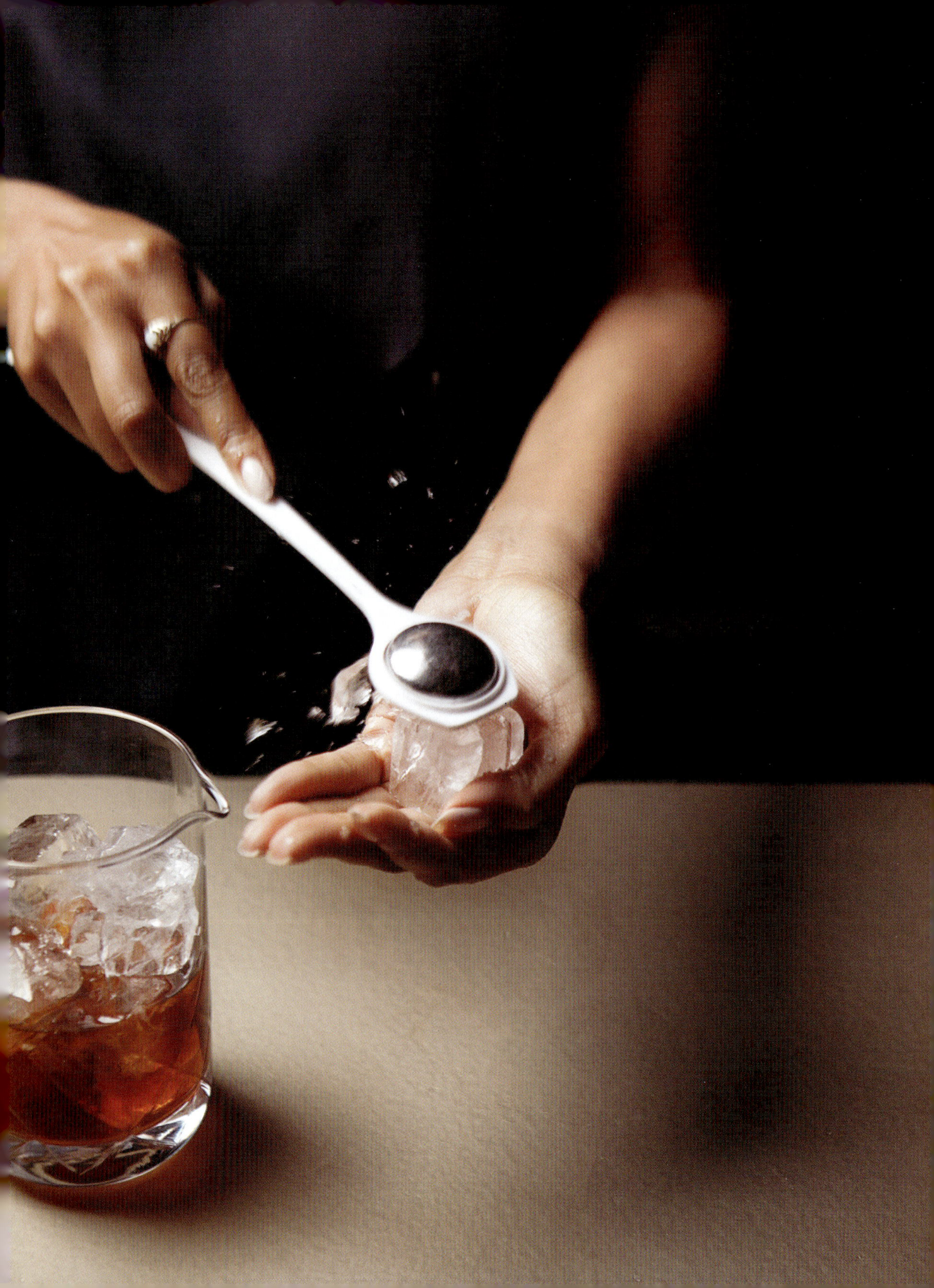

ANATOMY
OF A NIGHTCAP

Prior to the contemporary cocktail renaissance, the nightcap was one drinking tradition reticent to change—if it wasn't strong and served neat, it just wasn't a proper bedtime send-off. Thankfully, the idea of what constitutes that last drink before last call has expanded.

Nowadays, everything from your classic glass of whiskey on the rocks to complex fortified wines to exotic liqueurs to a cold canned beer with a shot on the side can count as your nightcap. There's really no concrete definition, so long as the drink helps you decompress and close out the night. "They're [there] to help . . . pull everything together," says Karri Cormican of San Francisco's Wildhawk.

Despite their frequent and welcome association with daytime drinking, herbal and floral liqueurs like *St-Germain* have found an unexpected foothold among professionals as a versatile nightcap tool, too. "It adds a nice, bright accent to typically overpowering things like Islay Scotch or mezcal," says PDT's Jim Meehan.

SERVES 1

Meaghan Dorman — Raines Law Room

MIDNIGHT BOUQUET

"A GREAT NIGHTCAP IS the perfect mix of strong and sweet," claims Meaghan Dorman, whose Midnight Bouquet incorporates *St-Germain* alongside grapefruit for a bittersweet companion to the salinity and smokiness of mezcal and tequila.

1 dash **Bitter Truth grapefruit bitters**
½ ounce **St-Germain**
¾ ounce **Amaro Averna**
¼ ounce **mezcal, preferably San Andrés Alipus**
1½ ounces **añejo tequila**

GLASS

GARNISH Grapefruit twist

METHOD Stir all of the ingredients in a mixing glass with ice. Strain into a coupe. Express the grapefruit twist over the surface and garnish.

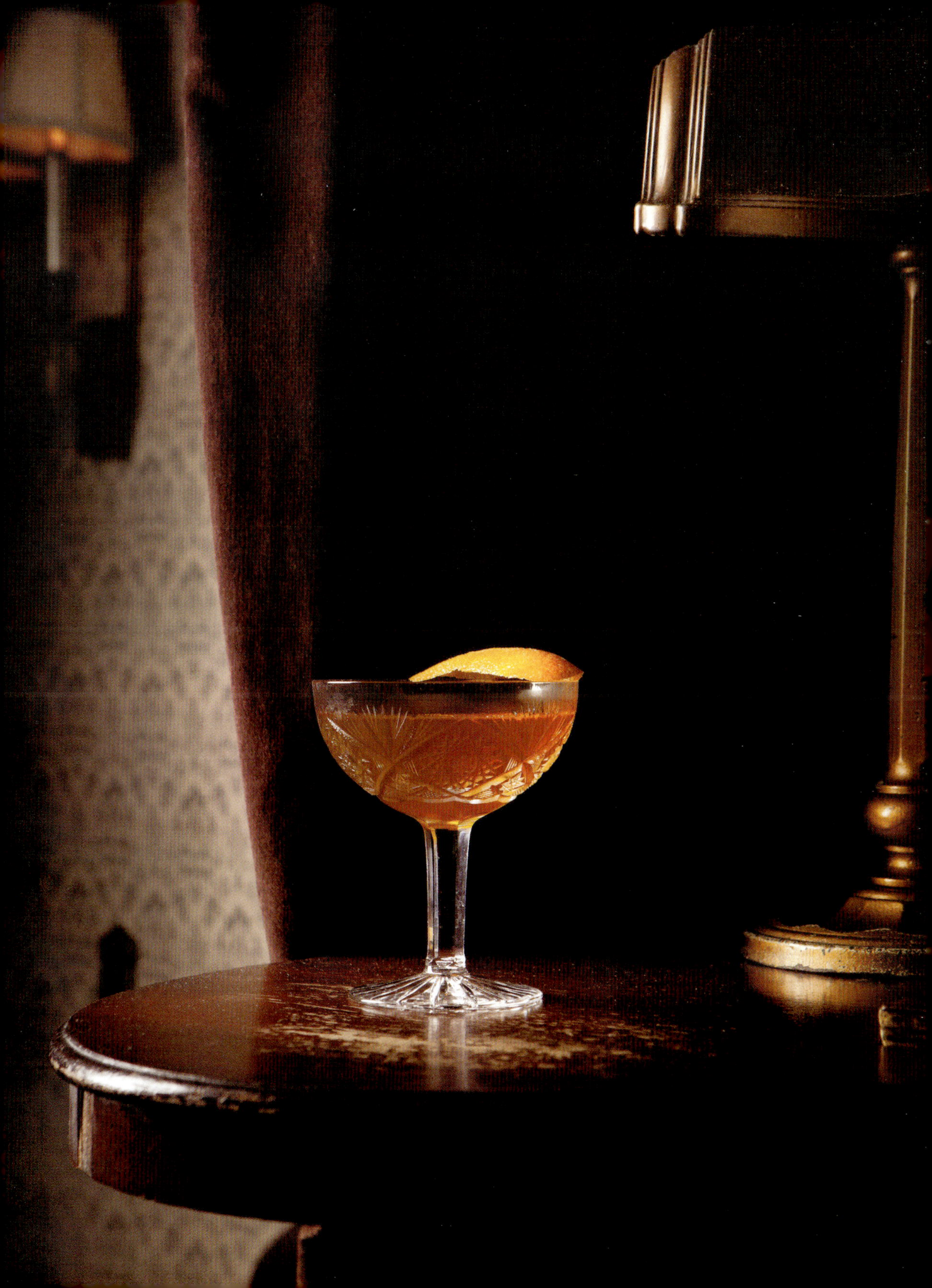

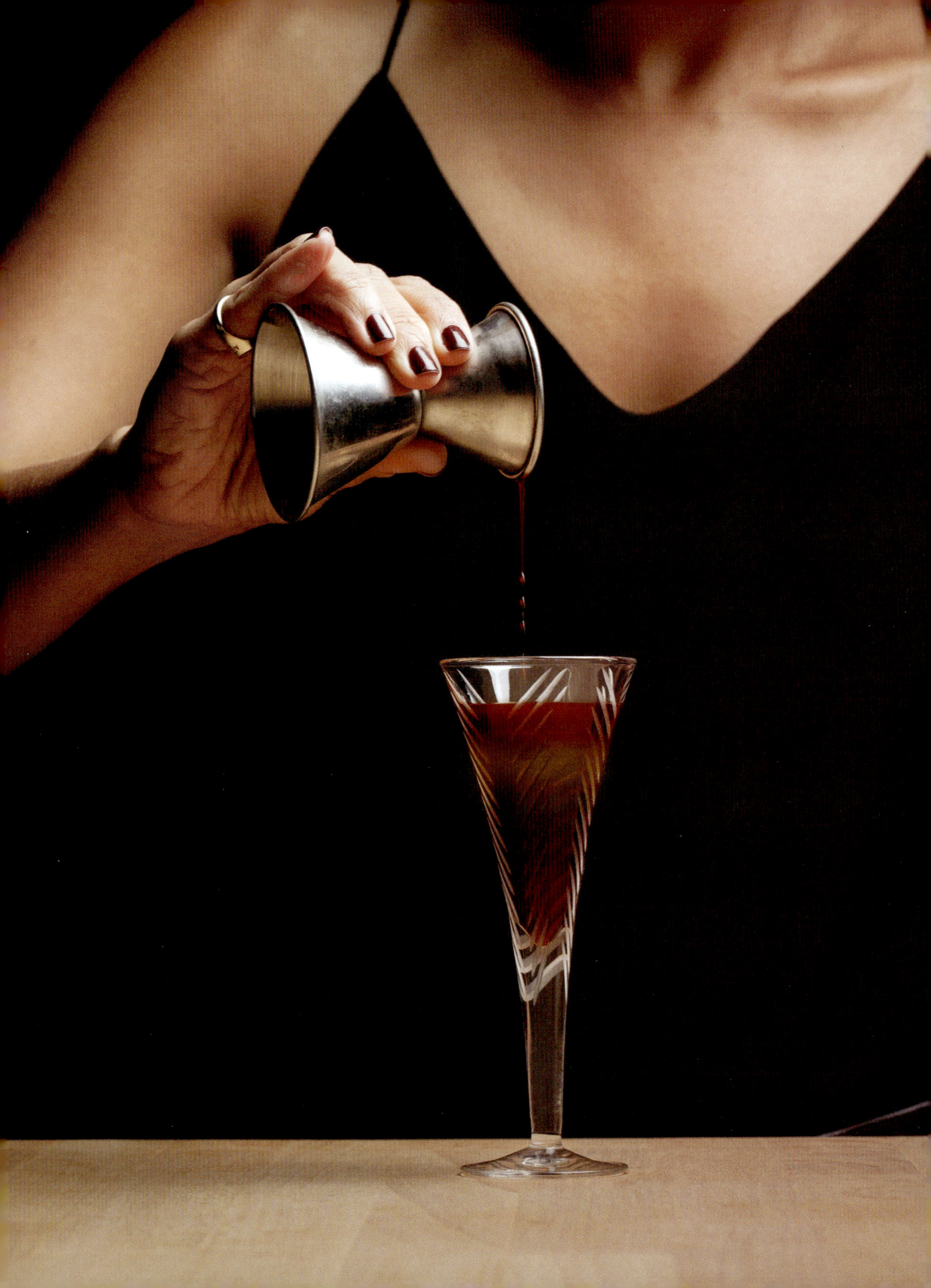

SERVES 1

Jamie Boudreau
—
Canon

COOPER'S
NIGHTCAP

JAMIE BOUDREAU'S NIGHTCAP IS meant to resolve a complex meal. The drink is versatile, "replicating an amaro for those times when one has a big dinner but the restaurant does not stock amari," explains Boudreau. "Most restaurants will have the three ingredients listed, and [thus] a happy stomach can now be had in most places."

½ ounce **chilled crème de mûre**
½ ounce **chilled *St-Germain***
½ ounce **chilled Angostura bitters**

GLASS

GARNISH None

METHOD Layer the ingredients in a shot glass in the order listed.

BUILDING A NIGHTCAP BAR

Building a proper home bar can be daunting, but prepping your house to accommodate any nightcap is a far simpler, and equally noble, pursuit.

- **SPIRITS:** Start simply by stocking base bottles. Whether it's whiskey, gin, mezcal, or tequila—if you enjoy sipping them neat, then they are nimble enough to mix, too. Raines Law Room bar director Meaghan Dorman recommends investing in a solid aged rum in this category as well. "A good aged rum is wonderful to sip on, and has that touch of sweetness and some lovely coffee, chocolate, and vanilla notes," she says. "They tend to be rich, and play well with amaro or vermouths, but also they are great on their own."

- **VERMOUTH AND SHERRY:** More delicate and nuanced than straight spirits, fortified wines may not scream "nightcap," but their immense versatility makes them an invaluable home bar tool. Stocking a sweet vermouth and an oloroso or amontillado sherry (both of which can be swapped in for sweet vermouth in classics) is a nightcap must. Just remember that fortified wines have a limited shelf life and fare best when kept cold.

- **LIQUEURS:** Amari can provide an easy riffing point—though drinking them straight is always a fine option, too. "Amari are practically cocktails in a bottle by themselves, so it won't get any easier," says Jamie Boudreau of Canon in Seattle. Elsewhere, herbal and floral liqueurs like Chartreuse, Suze, or *St-Germain* are important additions to the nightcap arsenal. "A lot of people like to finish their night with a cocktail instead of a straight spirit," says PDT's Jim Meehan, referring to the role of these liqueurs as more complex sweeteners in drinks like, say, the Old-Fashioned. "And for those people, *St-Germain* works as a great modifier—a nice accent to some of those more powerful spirits."

- **AROMATIC BITTERS:** With their innumerable applications, a bottle each of Angostura and Peychaud's bitters provide the "seasoning" a home bar requires. But the world of bitters is vast, so don't limit yourself. Stocking a larger range of bitters—from orange to lavender to smoked chile—is a simple way to add aromatic complexity and a whisper of bitterness to any nightcap.

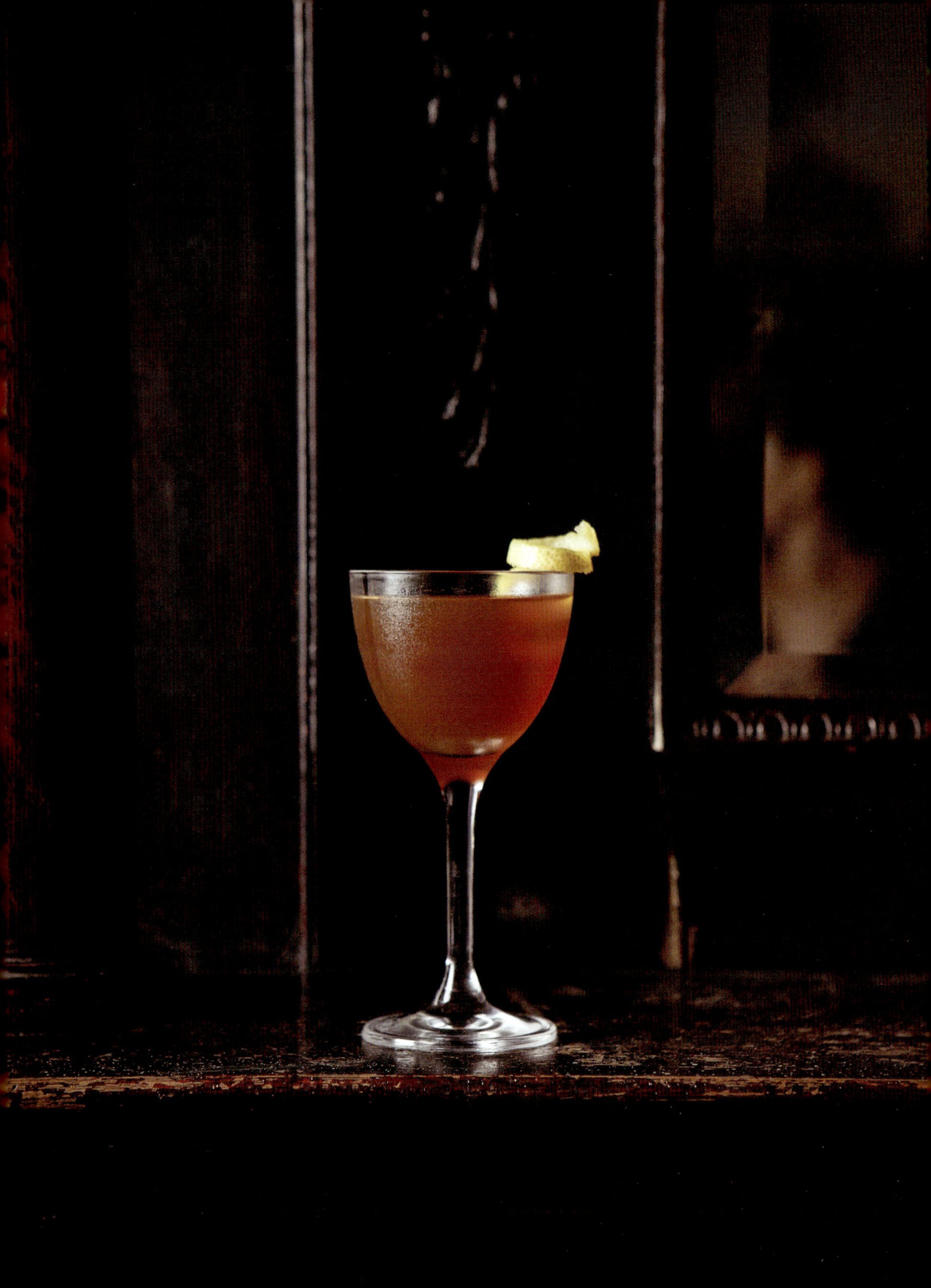

SERVES 1

Kimberly Rosselle

Trick Dog

LICKETY
SPLIT

DRAWING FROM THE INGREDIENTS that she herself would most want at the end of the night, Kimberly Rosselle pairs dry vermouth with the floral notes of *St-Germain* and the bitterness of Amaro Lucano, combining "Bold, bright flavors ... with delicate floral notes to soothe and relax one before wrapping up the night."

1 ounce **dry vermouth**
¾ ounce **St-Germain**
¾ ounce **Amaro Lucano**

GLASS

GARNISH Lemon peel

METHOD Add all ingredients to a mixing glass, add ice, and stir. Strain into a Nick & Nora glass, and garnish with the lemon peel.

SERVES 1

Jim Meehan
—
PDT

DUBOUDREAU
COCKTAIL

JIM MEEHAN UPDATES THE rye-based Cooper Cocktail created by Seattle's renowned Jamie Boudreau (see Cooper's Nightcap, page 141) in an East Coast ode to the West Coast original. The addition of Dubonnet adds an herbal, spicy-sweet element to the bittersweet combo of Fernet Branca and *St-Germain*.

2 ounces **rye whiskey, preferably Rittenhouse**
¾ ounce **Dubonnet Rouge**
¼ ounce **Fernet Branca**
¼ ounce *St-Germain*

GLASS

GARNISH Lemon twist

METHOD Add all ingredients to a mixing glass, add ice, and stir. Strain into a coupe and garnish with the lemon twist.

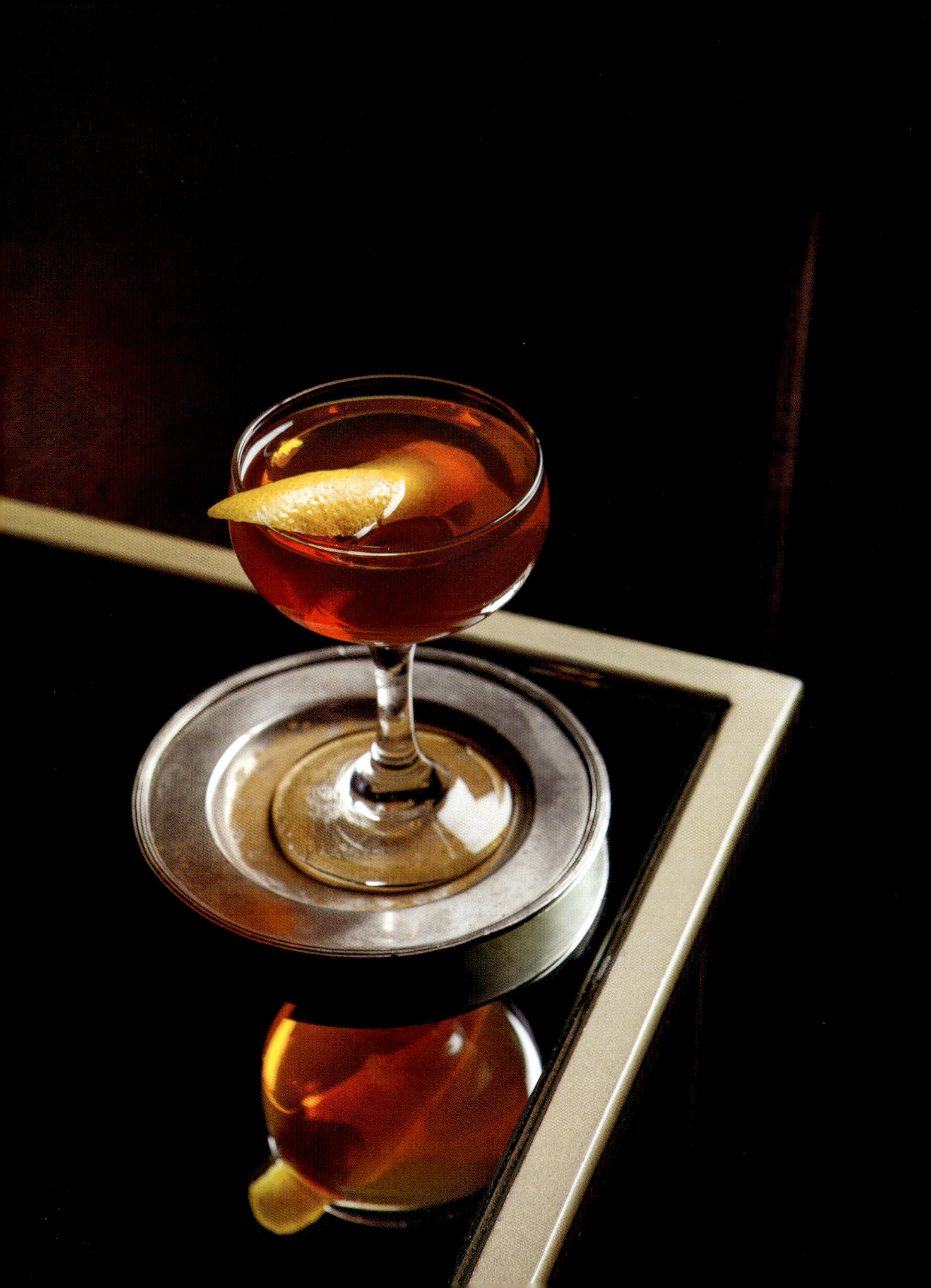

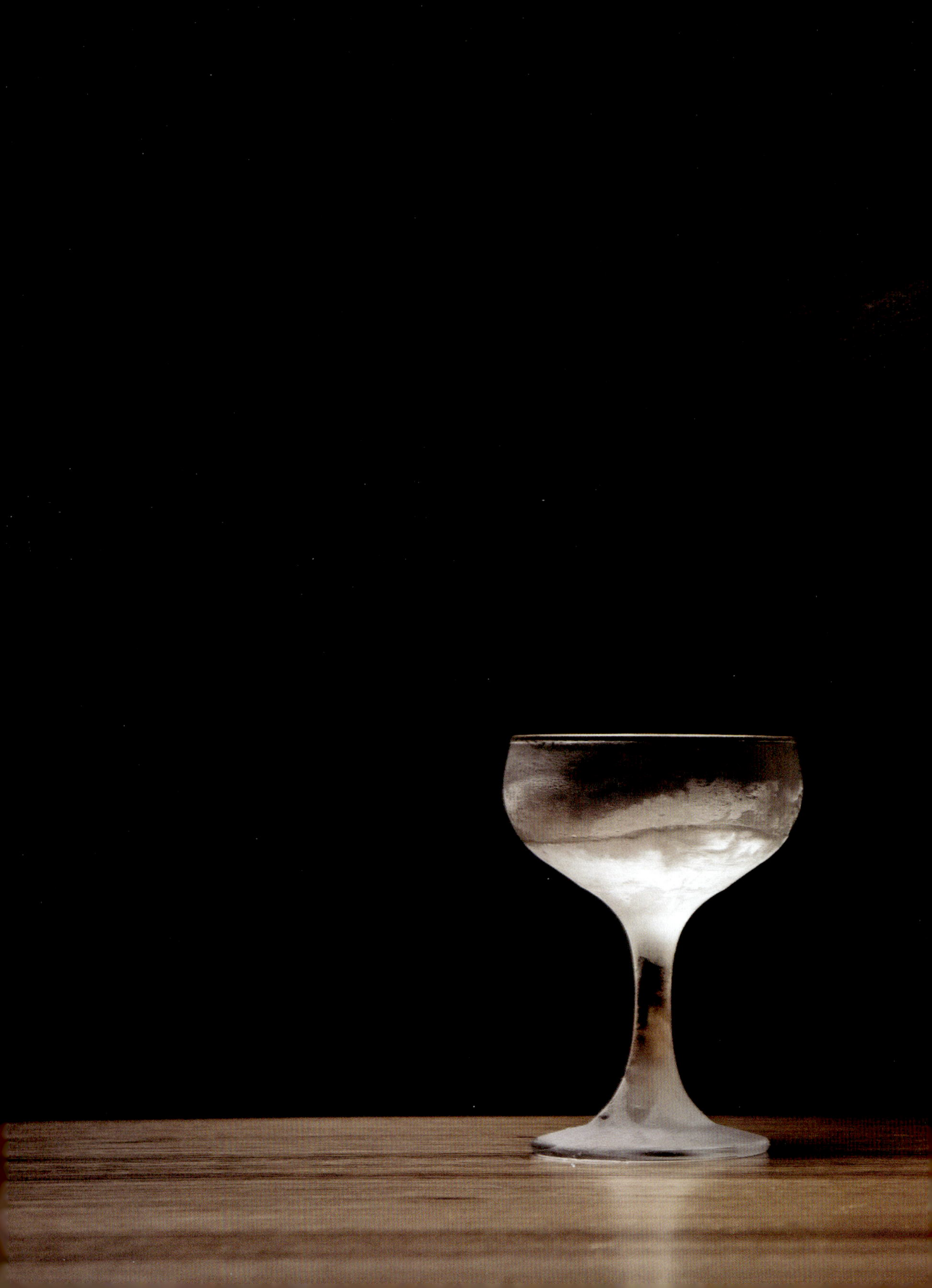

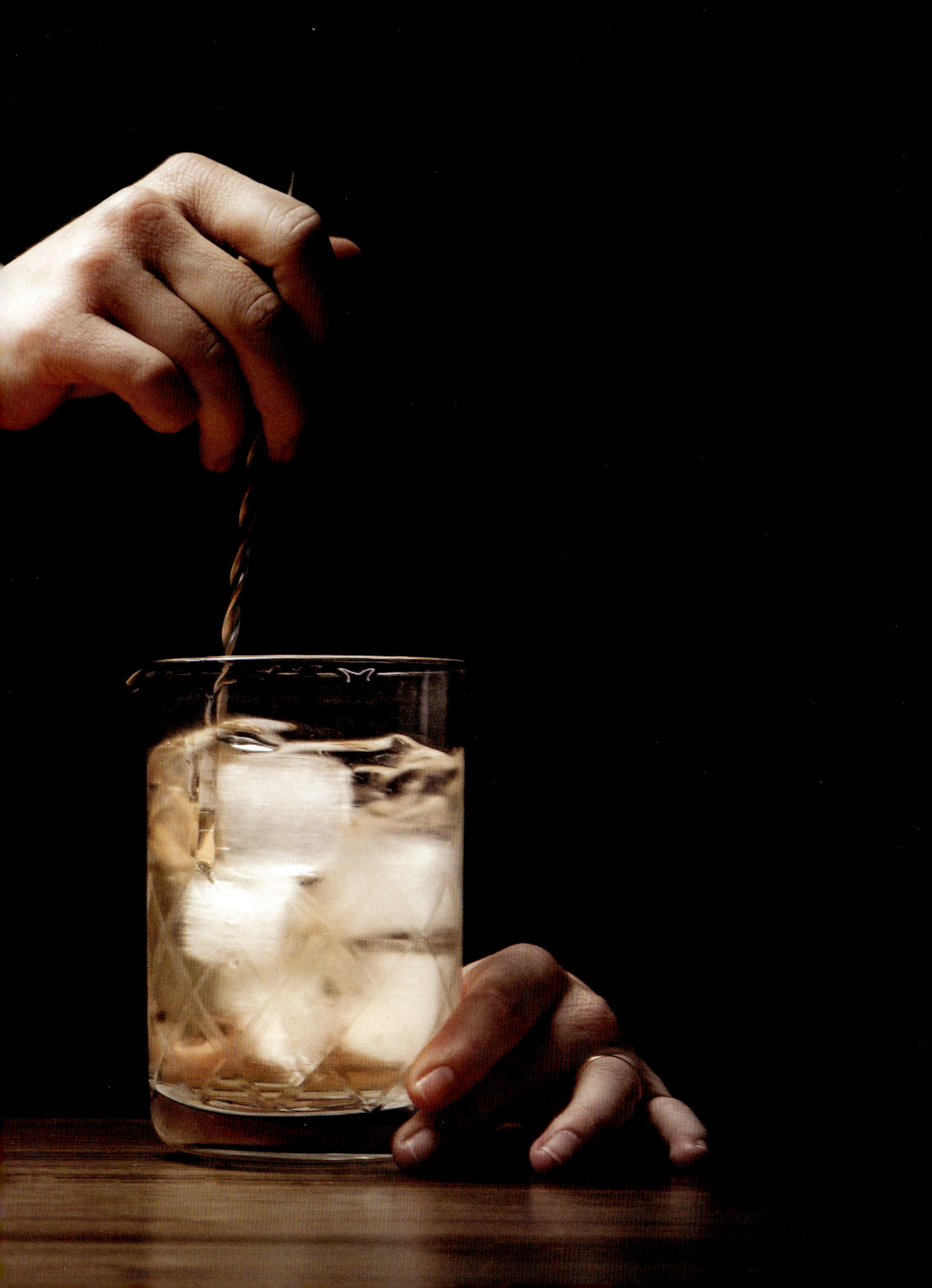

BRUNCH
SHRUBS AND SYRUPS

GEWÜRTZTRAMINER SYRUP

In a saucepan, heat **1 (750 ml) bottle gewürtztraminer** over medium-high heat until reduced by half. Add **12 ounces sugar** to the hot liquid. Stir to combine thoroughly, and bottle. Will keep in the fridge for up to 1 week.

STRAWBERRY SYRUP

Quarter **2 quarts whole strawberries** (thawed, if frozen), drop them into a bowl, and sprinkle with **3 cups cane sugar**. Let sit for 1 hour. Transfer the mixture to a saucepan and add **2 cups water**. Heat over medium heat for 30 minutes, or until the strawberries get very light in color and look mushy. Let cool at room temperature. Will keep in the fridge for up to 1 week.

MUÑA SYRUP

Place **2 tablespoons dried *muña* (or dried peppermint tea)** in a quart container. Add hot water and steep for 10 minutes. Strain, then add **2 cups sugar**. Stir until the sugar has dissolved. Will keep in the fridge for up to 1 week.

STRAWBERRY SHRUB

In a saucepan, combine **2 cups chopped strawberries**, **1 cup red wine vinegar**, **2 cups sugar**, and **1 cup water**. Bring to a simmer, stirring to dissolve the sugar, for 20 minutes. Let cool. Strain out the strawberries (save them for later use, if desired). Will keep in the fridge for up to 1 month.

DAYTIME

SYRUPS

HONEYDEW SYRUP

Peel and seed **one honeydew melon.** Pass the melon through a juicer or puree in a blender and strain through a fine-mesh sieve into a bowl. Add **equal parts sugar** by volume. Stir or shake until the sugar has dissolved. Store in an airtight container in the fridge for up to 4 days. (One melon yields 2 cups of juice. With sugar, it yields approximately 3½ cups of syrup.)

GINGER SYRUP

Pass a **ginger root** through a juicer and measure ½ cup of the juice (reserve the remainder for another use). Transfer to a saucepan and add **8 ounces sugar** and **½ cup water**. Heat over low heat, stirring, until the sugar has dissolved. Will keep in the fridge for up to 1 week.

STRAWBERRY SYRUP

Hull and quarter **12 medium strawberries**. Place them in a saucepan with **2 cups water** and bring to a simmer. Add **16 ounces sugar** and simmer, stirring, until the sugar has dissolved. Remove from the heat and let cool for 30 minutes. Strain into a storage container and let cool completely. Will keep in the fridge for up to 1 week.

APERITIF
SYRUPS AND JUICES

KIWI SYRUP

Puree **3 kiwis** in a blender. Strain the puree through a coffee filter into a measuring cup. Add an equal quantity of **sugar** and stir to combine. Transfer to a saucepan and heat over medium heat, stirring, until the sugar has dissolved. Will keep in the fridge for up to 1 week.

CUCUMBER JUICE

Peel a **cucumber** and pass it through a juicer, cutting it down to fit, if necessary. Strain the juice through a fine-mesh sieve to remove any remaining solids. Will keep in the fridge for up to 6 days.

LEMON CORDIAL

Add **1 ounce of vodka** to the **zest of 10 lemons**, and set aside. In a large container, combine **2 cups of sugar** with **2 cups of lemon juice**. Add the vodka and lemon zest mixture, cover, and set aside overnight to infuse. Fine strain, bottle, and store. Will keep for up to 1 month in the fridge.

DINNER

SYRUPS AND MORE

ST-GERMAIN ELDERFLOWER ICE CUBES

In a spouted measuring cup, combine **2 ounces St-Germain**, **¾ ounce lemon juice**, and **1½ ounces water**. Pour into an ice cube tray and freeze until solid.

SMOKED TOMATO-INFUSED ST-GERMAIN

Place **4 ounces smoked tomatoes** in a sterilized 2-quart glass jar. Pour in **1 (750 ml) bottle St-Germain**. Set aside to infuse for 5 days. Strain and transfer to a clean jar or bottle. Will keep in the fridge for up to 2 months.

AGAVE SYRUP

Combine equal quantities of **agave nectar** and **water**. Stir until the agave has dissolved. Will keep for 1 year at room temperature.

MINT TEA

In a mug or glass measuring cup, steep **1 tablespoon loose mint tea** in **1 cup boiling water** for 4 to 5 minutes. Strain and let cool to room temperature.

ST-GERMAIN SORBET

In a bowl, stir together **¼ cup St-Germain**, **¼ cup simple syrup**, **¼ cup lemon juice**, **½ cup water**, and **1 tablespoon crushed pink peppercorns**. Refrigerate the sorbet base until cold. Transfer to an ice cream maker and process into sorbet according to the manufacturer's instructions. Transfer to a storage container and freeze overnight.

INDEX

A
Ace Hotel, 10, 35, 39
agave syrup, 153
Al Fresco Spritz, 78
Alta Linea, 82
Amaro Averna
　Midnight Bouquet, 138
Amaro Lucano
　Lickety Split, 145
Amaro Montenegro
　C Vidal, 64
Americano, 82
aperitifs
　Al Fresco Spritz, 78
　in America, 82
　appeal of, 58, 61
　custom of, 58–59
　C Vidal, 64
　drink categories for, 59–60
　etymology of, 58
　Gentleman Caller, 86
　at home, 92–93
　low-proof cocktails and, 68
　Lysette, 70
　Qui Oui?, 81
　Rivington Punch, 63
　rules of, 75
　The *St-Germain* Cocktail, 90
　A Scented Stretch, 73
　sessionability and, 60
　The Shining Path, 85
　Tête-à-Tête, 95
Aperol
　Gentleman Caller, 86
　Qui Oui?, 81
　Rivington Punch, 63
Arenella, Michael, 48
Attaboy, 127, 135
Avèze gentian liqueur
　The Shining Path, 85
The Aviary, 10, 104, 109, 111

B
Barnacle, 82
Beattie, Scott, 104
Beringer, Guy, 14, 18
Best, Greg, 10, 60, 68, 73
Biancaniello, Matthew, 101, 105, 114
Big Star, 15, 30
Bodenheimer, Neal, 10, 35, 40, 44
Bordeleau, Jay, 117, 118
Boudreau, Jamie, 127–28, 141, 142, 146
bourbon
　Grievous Angel, 30
　Voodoo Down, 106
Brennan, Georgeanne, 59
Broken Shaker, 47
brunch
　appeal of, 18
　drink categories for, 15, 17, 18, 25
　East of Eden, 21
　etymology of, 14
　Grievous Angel, 30
　history of, 14–15
　Señorita Spritz, 22
　Tiger Beat, 29

C
cachaça
　Da Hora, 50
Café Henri, 10, 35, 40
Cane & Table, 10, 35, 40
Canon, 127, 141, 142
cava
　Da Hora, 50
　Señorita Spritz, 22

DRINK FRENCH FLUENTLY ◆ 154

Champagne
    The *St-Germain* Cocktail, 90
Chartreuse
    The Hudson Glacier, 118
Clover Club, 10, 15, 18, 48, 53
Clyde Common, 10, 15, 25
Cocchi Americano
    The Hudson Glacier, 118
    Surf City Spritz, 39
Compère Lapin, 86, 99, 111, 116
Cooper's Nightcap, 141
Cormican, Karri, 127, 131, 132
Cox, Julian, 98, 116
crème de mûre
    Cooper's Nightcap, 141
cucumber juice, 152
culinary cocktails, 104–5
Curaçao
    Darlin' Don't Refrain, 109
Cure, 10, 35, 40, 44
C Vidal, 64
Cynar
    Fiore di Francia, 121

D

Da Hora, 50
Dante, 78, 82
Darlin' Don't Refrain, 109
Daroco, 81
David, Natasha, 10, 60, 63
Davis, Miles, 106
Day, Alex, 59, 60, 68, 82
day drinking
    appeal of, 34, 35
    by city, 40
    Da Hora, 50
    Flapper's Delight, 53
    For Rex, 44
    Nudie Beach, 47
    San Pancho, 36
    sessionability and, 35
    Surf City Spritz, 39
    venues for, 35, 40
de Soto, Nico, 81, 101
dinner cocktails
    collaboration and, 98–99, 101
    culinary influence on, 104–5
    Darlin' Don't Refrain, 109
    Fiore di Francia, 121
    The Hudson Glacier, 118
    Keystone Highball, 113
    mise en place and, 110–11
    pairing food and, 116–17
    Smoked Tomato, 114
    Voodoo Down, 106
Dionysos, Marco, 104
Dorman, Meaghan, 138, 142
Drink, 99, 110, 121
Dubonnet Rouge
    Duboudreau Cocktail, 146

E

East of Eden, 21
elderflower ice cubes, 153
Eleven Madison Park, 10, 98, 106, 117
Elliott, Will, 85, 99, 116
Evans, Marta Jean, 29

F

Fernet Branca
    Duboudreau Cocktail, 146
    Sailin' On, 132
Fiore di Francia, 121
Flapper's Delight, 53
Flatiron Lounge, 15, 48
For Rex, 44

G

Galliano Ristretto
    Sailin' On, 132
Gentleman Caller, 86

gewütztraminer syrup, 150
gin
    Al Fresco Spritz, 78
    Darlin' Don't Refrain, 109
    East of Eden, 21
    Flapper's Delight, 53
    Gentleman Caller, 86
    The Hudson Glacier, 118
    Nudie Beach, 47
    San Pancho, 36
    Señorita Spritz, 22
    Surf City Spritz, 39
    Tête-à-Tête, 95
ginger syrup, 151
Greenbaum, Dan, 127, 128, 135
GreenRiver, 104, 105, 113, 117
Grievous Angel, 30
Griffiths, Brian, 47
Gullo, Abigail, 86, 99, 111, 116

H

Herit, Xavier, 17, 25, 95
honeydew syrup, 151
The Hudson Glacier, 118
Humm, Daniel, 98

J

Jazz Age Lawn Party, 48, 53

K

Keystone Highball, 113
kiwi syrup, 152
Kline, Harry May, 39

L

lager
    Lysette, 70
Laman, Caitlin, 36, 40
Lebec, Laurent, 15, 30
Le Boudoir, 60, 70
Lettuce Entertain You, 98, 116
Leyenda, 34, 50
Lickety Split, 145
Lillet Blanc
    Tiger Beat, 29
Llama Inn, 17, 25
Longman & Eagle, 29
low-proof cocktail movement, 68
Lysette, 70

M

Mace, 81, 99
Madeira
    C Vidal, 64
Maison Premiere, 10, 85, 99, 116
Marrero, Lynnette, 17, 22, 25
Marshall, Franky, 60, 70
Maurin Quina
    The Shining Path, 85
Maven, 117, 118
McDonnell, Duggan, 104
Meehan, Jim, 126, 127, 131, 139, 146
Melton, Micah, 104, 109, 111
Menton, 99
mezcal
    Midnight Bouquet, 138
mint tea, 153
mise en place, 110–11
Mix, Ivy, 34–35, 50
Momose, Julia, 104, 105, 113, 117
Morand, Paul, 59
Morgenthaler, Jeffrey, 10, 15, 21, 25
muña syrup, 150

N

nightcaps
    Cooper's Nightcap, 143
    drink categories of, 126–28, 131
    Duboudreau Cocktail, 146
    home bar for, 142–143
    importance of, 126

Lickety Split, 145
Midnight Bouquet, 138
Sailin' On, 132
tradition of, 126
Turn Down Service, 135
Nitecap, 10, 60, 63, 82
NoMad Hotel, 98, 117
Nudie Beach, 47
No. 9 Park, 99

O

Ojen
    For Rex, 44

P

pairings, 116–17
PDT, 126, 131, 139, 146
port
    Turn Down Service, 135
Prosecco
    Al Fresco Spritz, 78
    Qui Oui?, 81

Q

Qui Oui?, 81

R

Raines Law Room, 142, 140
raspberry liqueur
    Rivington Punch, 63
Reiner, Julie, 10, 15, 18, 48, 53
Rivington Punch, 63
Robitschek, Leo, 98, 106, 117
rosé wine
    Rivington Punch, 63
Rosselle, Kimberly, 127, 145
rum
    for nightcaps, 142
    A Scented Stretch, 73
    Surf City Spritz, 39
    Voodoo Down, 106
rye whiskey
    Duboudreau Cocktail, 146

S

Sabo, Dan, 10, 35, 39, 40
Sailin' On, 132
St-Germain
    Al Fresco Spritz, 78
    Cooper's Nightcap, 143
    C Vidal, 64
    Da Hora, 50
    Darlin' Don't Refrain, 109
    Duboudreau Cocktail, 146
    East of Eden, 21
    elderflower ice cubes, 153
    Fiore di Francia, 121
    Flapper's Delight, 53
    For Rex, 44
    Gentleman Caller, 86
    Grievous Angel, 30
    The Hudson Glacier, 118
    Keystone Highball, 113
    Lickety Split, 145
    Lysette, 70
    Midnight Bouquet, 138
    Nudie Beach, 47
    Qui Oui?, 81
    Rivington Punch, 63
    Sailin' On, 132
    The *St-Germain* Cocktail, 90
    San Pancho, 36
    A Scented Stretch, 73
    Señorita Spritz, 22
    The Shining Path, 85
    Smoked Tomato, 114
    smoked tomato-infused, 153
    sorbet, 153
    Surf City Spritz, 39
    Tête-à-Tête, 95
    Tiger Beat, 29
    Turn Down Service, 135
    Voodoo Down, 106
Salers gentian liqueur
    Lysette, 70
    The Shining Path, 85

San Pancho, 36
Sauvage, 99, 116
A Scented Stretch, 73
Scotch whisky
    Fiore di Francia, 121
    Turn Down Service, 135
Señorita Spritz, 22
sherry
    Darlin' Don't Refrain, 109
    Gentleman Caller, 86
    for nightcaps, 138
    San Pancho, 36
    Señorita Spritz, 22
The Shining Path, 85
shrub, strawberry, 150
Smoked Tomato, 114
sorbet, St-Germain, 153
sparkling wine. See also individual wines
    The Hudson Glacier, 118
Star, Ezra, 99, 110, 121
strawberries
    shrub, 150
    syrup, 150, 151
Surf City Spritz, 39

syrups
    agave, 153
    gewützträminer, 150
    ginger, 151
    honeydew, 151
    kiwi, 152
    muña, 150
    strawberry, 150, 151

T

tea, mint, 153
tequila
    Midnight Bouquet, 140
Tête-à-Tête, 95
Ticonderoga Club, 60, 68, 73
Tiger Beat, 29
Trick Dog, 36, 127, 145
Turn Down Service, 135

V

vermouth
    Al Fresco Spritz, 78
    Lickety Split, 145
    for nightcaps, 138
Vidal, Camille, 9, 59, 60, 64, 90
vodka
    Tiger Beat, 29
    Voodoo Down, 106

W

Wallflower, 17, 25, 95
whiskey. See also bourbon; rye whiskey; Scotch whisky
    Keystone Highball, 113
white wine
    A Scented Stretch, 73
Wildhawk, 127, 131, 132
Wiznitzer, Pamela, 64

Y

Young, Naren, 59–60, 61, 78, 82

Text copyright © 2016 by PUNCH Creative
Photographs copyright © 2016 by PUNCH Creative

All rights reserved.

Published in the United States by PUNCH Creative,
a branded content studio of PUNCH, a registered trademark of
Penguin Random House LLC.

punchdrink.com

All trademarks are trademarks of their respective owners.

Printed in the United States of America

Cover and interior design by Laura Palese

Icon illustrations by Haisam Hussein

10 9 8 7 6 5 4 3 2 1

First Edition

PUNCH Creative is an in-house custom content studio in affiliation with PUNCH (punchdrink.com), an online magazine and imprint of Ten Speed Press. With a team of writers, editors, photographers, and videographers, PUNCH Creative produces a range of innovative partnered content across a variety of platforms on the web and in print. From books to video, our work reflects our commitment to narrative journalism, original stories, and stunning visuals while tapping into our deep knowledge of the drinks space, spectrum of production capabilities, and singular aesthetic.

CAMILLE RALPH VIDAL, also known as Madame St-Germain, is the global ambassador for premium French liqueur *St-Germain*. A native of southern France, she has worked at high-end bars across the globe, including Experimental Cocktail Club in London and Golden Monkey in Melbourne. Today, she works to spread her love for the award-winning elderflower liqueur, sharing her passion for and knowledge of the art of the aperitif and the versatility of *St-Germain* with consumers and bartenders around the world.